P L A T O :

T O T A L I T A R I A N
O R   D E M O C R A T ?

Essays Selected and Introduced by
Thomas Landon Thorson

A SPECTRUM BOOK

PRENTICE-HALL, INC., Englewood Cliffs, N.J.

Library of Congress Catalog Card Number: 63-15936

PRINTED IN THE UNITED STATES OF AMERICA—C

To my mother

Table of
CONTENTS

INTRODUCTION

Thomas Landon Thorson

There are perhaps no writings in the history of Western thought which deserve the adjective "classic" more than those of Plato. If the test of a classic is its continuing relevance to contemporary problems, Plato's work, and especially the *Republic*, must be given a very high score indeed. The pages following are ample testimony to the significance of Plato for twentieth-century politics.

But Plato has by no means simply been given the reverence due a notable figure long since dead. For the past twenty-five years or so his writings have been the subject of vigorous, even virulent, controversy. The fact of this controversy is perhaps the prime evidence of the timelessness of his thought. The point at issue, precipitated undoubtedly by the emergence of totalitarianism alongside liberal democracy in the Western tradition, is whether Plato is to be understood as the forefather of totalitarianism or of democracy. Prior to the development of the full power of Hitler and Stalin the latter interpretation rather clearly held sway, but in recent years the former view has become almost orthodox.

The details of the dispute have hitherto been concealed from the general reader and the general, but not professional, student of Plato

Thomas Landon Thorson *is Associate Professor of Political Science, University of Wisconsin. He was graduated with honors from Indiana University and holds a Ph.D. from Princeton University. Having contributed a number of articles to scholarly journals, he is also the author of* The Logic of Democracy *and in 1962-63 held a Guggenheim Fellowship for study at Oxford.*

by the forbidding size and often technical titles of the works in which they are contained. To help to remedy this situation is one of the major objectives of this volume. To help the student and general reader achieve a profounder understanding of Plato is, however, its greater purpose.

There is also another purpose. To read Plato with genuine understanding is to come to grips with the problems of political philosophy. What makes his writing significant is not, certainly, that Plato solves all the problems, but that he raises most of them. The ideological struggle in which we are presently engaged is not, as we are often led to believe, a matter of who can produce the most rolled steel or string beans. It is more nearly a matter of choosing between an open and a closed society—as one of our authors would put it—or between natural law and naked power—as another would formulate it. This book is a kind of seven-way dialogue among Plato and the six authors on most of the important questions of the contemporary "war of ideas." Since neither the answers nor the questions are simple, the reader will be obliged to make it an eight-sided conversation.

On the whole it seems to me most useful to allow, in so far as possible, the various disputants to speak for themselves. I have, therefore, presented here substantial portions of the argument of each author. It will, however, even at the risk of a certain over-simplification be helpful to many readers to erect a tentative intellectual framework in terms of which the controversy concerning Plato can be viewed.

The first fact to which I should like to call attention is an obvious one, but no less important for this reason. The Plato controversy here presented takes place *inside* the liberal democratic tradition. All of the contributors are longtime residents of either the United States or Great Britain. They all are personally and intellectually supporters of democracy against totalitarianism. Given this common political faith, it might be reasonable to expect them to join together either in opposition to Plato, the embryonic totalitarian, or in support of Plato, the embryonic democrat. But no such general alliance exists. On the contrary, as the reader will discover, the division into opposers and supporters is firm and the differences of opinion razor sharp.

It is not at all persuasive to explain this division by arguing that Plato's writings are simply ambiguous. Plato surely is a many-sided thinker, but he is just as surely not ambiguous in the ordinary sense that statements like "It's a nice day" or "She's a professional" are ambiguous. Indeed, for critics like Karl Popper there is no ambiguity —Plato is simply a totalitarian—and for other commentators Plato is just as simply not a totalitarian.

One can, it seems to me, come close to an adequate explanation of these contrary interpretations by looking for a moment not at Plato but at the commentators' conceptions of democracy and totalitarianism. I have suggested that they are all supporters of democracy. Thus, we can be sure that they all would react similarly to what might be called the physical attributes of democratic and totalitarian regimes. They would, in other words, favor regular free elections, freedom of speech and of the press, and constitutional restrictions on police activity; and they would with equal vigor oppose one-party elections, censorship, and concentration camps. But agreement on desirable and undesirable characteristics of actual societies by no means demands agreement on the theoretical foundations for these characteristics.

Raising the question of theoretical foundations gets us to the heart of the matter. The interpretations of Plato contained in this volume do not dispute the respective virtues of democracy and totalitarianism, for, as we have noted, they are all written by supporters of democracy. The real question at issue is "Do the theoretical foundations supplied to the Western tradition by Plato give support to totalitarianism or to democracy?" It is this central focus of the dispute that makes it important. Engaging in historical research for the purpose of discovering what a writer dead for over 2000 years "really meant" by his words is not without significance, but it is much more significant to illuminate issues which are very much alive. The discussion here is in large measure a discussion in contemporary political theory or political philosophy, and Plato's *Republic* is a timeless classic because it can serve as the locus for such a discussion.

It has frequently been suggested in recent years that political philosophy as a "going concern" is dead, that scholars instead of actively writing political philosophy bury themselves in the irrelevancy of ancient texts. The character of the Plato controversy casts considerable doubt on both parts of this allegation.

What is this argument over theoretical foundations that I have mentioned all about? We can begin to get an answer to this question by thinking about what we mean by the word "democracy." Suppose we were to ask a group of Americans about the meaning of democracy. Someone would say, "Democracy means majority rule." Others might suggest "rule by the people," "equality," and "individual freedom." If we asked a teacher of political theory, he would be likely to say the same thing in more technical language: "Democracy is a political system operating on the principles of majority rule, popular sovereignty, political equality, and the protection of individual and minority political rights."

To say this, however, is only to give a reasonably adequate description of what, so to speak, a democracy looks like. Such a definition merely suggests and by no means solves certain theoretical and practical questions of greatest importance to the operation of democratic government. In many ways the central problem of democracy is the question of the proper relationship between the principle of majority rule on the one hand and the principle of the protection of individual and minority rights on the other. This is, of course, a problem of great practical significance in the history of democratic government, particularly in the United States. The Northern anti-slavery majority v. the property rights of the Southern minority. The white Southern majority v. the rights of the black minority. The monogamous majority v. the polygamous Mormon minority. We would not be hard-pressed to name a score of similar examples, but our interest here is not so much in the practical problem as in the theoretical one.

Consideration of the practical problem can, however, help us focus upon important aspects of the theoretical problem. In 1932 Franklin D. Roosevelt was elected President of the United States by a substantial majority and the Democratic Party achieved large majorities in both the Senate and the House of Representatives. Without much doubt this was a mandate for the Democrats to deal with the economic depression which had begun in 1929. A great many economic measures were passed by Congress and signed by President Roosevelt in the years that followed 1932. Many of the new laws were designed to regulate the use of property and wealth, and a considerable portion of them were declared unconstitutional by the Supreme Court on the grounds that the regulations infringed upon the rights of individuals to the free use of their property. Both sides contended that "democracy" was on their side.

When this dispute is analyzed, it is possible to see two quite different conceptions of democracy emerging from it. Roosevelt, on the one side, saw democracy principally as the freedom of the majority, through its elected representatives, to adopt policies which would solve its problems. The majority of the Court, former President Herbert Hoover, and a good many others saw democracy primarily as protection of the rights of individuals against the power of government even when that government represented the will of the majority. All this is, however, not to say that Roosevelt rejected the rights of individuals or that the Supreme Court denied the principle of majority rule. The difference is rather a matter of emphasis.

This example is particularly useful in bringing into focus the fact that there can be and are two rather distinct kinds of democrats. There are what might be called "majority-rule democrats," those who see democracy primarily as an instrument to allow the mass of the people to rule themselves. "Individual-rights democrats" on the other hand see democracy as limited government, as a set of restrictions on government activity for the purpose of insuring maximum freedom for individuals. Again let me emphasize a point which will become clearer in a moment: these two types of supporters of democracy simply emphasize one principle, they do not in either case exclude the other principle.

The reader may, by this time, be wondering what all this has to do with the interpretation of Plato. To get the answer we must push a little further. Two closely related questions are in order: (1) What are the historical origins of democratic ideas? (2) What are the philosophical grounds for democracy? There is no single, simple answer to either of these questions and it is this fact which largely explains the differing conceptions of democracy just reviewed.

Speaking generally, one can as a matter of history point to two intellectual sources of democracy. One of them is the Classical-Christian conception of a higher or natural law. The ancient Greeks and Romans, particularly Plato, Aristotle, the Stoics, and Cicero, held that there existed an eternal and immutable source of values, an ultimate standard of right and wrong which could be discovered by rational man. Christianity, of course, posited the existence of a single omniscient and omnipotent God whose will provided an ultimate standard and source of values for men. These two traditions which began in antithesis ultimately merged, particularly in the teachings of the Roman Catholic Church. This synthesis was for many centuries, and in some measure continues to be, the dominant intellectual orientation of Western civilization. From this source, albeit over a very tortuous path, an argument for democratic government ultimately emerged. In very crude summary the argument goes like this:

> All men are created in the image of God.
> Therefore, all men are possessed with individual dignity.
> Thus, all men are created equal and are endowed with certain inalienable rights.
> Therefore, democratic government.

This argument tends to lay stress on the individual, his dignity and his rights, and majority rule enters only as a kind of secondary principle. Majority rule is in this context largely a sort of practical solution to the problem raised by the fact that a functioning government demands that someone be empowered to make decisions. To give decision-making power to one man or some group of men would be to violate the principle that all men are equal, but since unanimity is as a practical matter impossible, the only sensible thing is to allow the majority to rule. But, of course, one should not give the majority too much room to operate; it is best to hedge the majority in with constitutional restrictions of various kinds.

The important thing to see here is that it is quite possible to support democracy from what, for want of a better term, can be called an absolutist conception of values. From this point of view democracy is the best form of government because it prevents the arbitrary exercise of power in violation of the absolute moral law. Laws passed by men, even if by a majority, are not the highest standard; a particular law is right only if it coincides with the ultimate law prescribed by God or Nature.

The second source of democratic ideas is the scientific attitude, or in philosophical terms what is called empiricism. Again speaking generally, the scientific attitude holds that man's knowledge is limited to what he can experience, to what he can test by the evidence of his senses. When this attitude is applied to the argument for democracy, it comes out something like this:

> No man or group of men can know what is ultimately right.
> In this sense, all men are created equal.
> The only test of what men should have is what most of them want.
> Therefore, men should govern themselves.
> Thus, majority rule and democratic government.

Although majority rule is the prime principle, individual rights are also important because only if the individual is allowed to be free can new ideas, which may turn out to be good ones, be produced. Thus, what we have here is an argument for democracy deriving its support not from the contention that values are absolute, but from the wholly contrary philosophical view that values are relative.

We are now well on the way to making some sense of the contrary interpretations of Plato, and in a moment we shall go still further by applying the same sort of analysis to totalitarianism. Before that is done, however, it is important to add certain qualifications to what has been said about the theory of democracy. First, democratic practice as it has developed in the United States and elsewhere is not simply the implementation of one or the other of the points of view discussed above; it is rather an extraordinarily complicated hybrid of both. Such analysis can be an aid in understanding, but it cannot account for everything that democracies do. Secondly, we have noted an association between philosophical absolutism and individual-rights democracy and between philosophical relativism and majority-rule democracy. This is on the whole sound, but it would be a mistake to think that these elements are necessarily connected in this way. Thus, philosophical absolutism and majority-rule democracy can be paired if it is assumed that absolute values reside not in the individual but in the group. Similarly, philosophical relativism can support an individual-rights conception of democracy if the masses are judged to be stupid and impulsive while intelligence and sound judgment is presumed to be the property of a few. The important thing is that democracy of whatever emphasis can be supported by either philosophical foundation.

Totalitarianism can plausibly be interpreted in terms of either leg of the absolutism-relativism dichotomy which we have found at the roots of democracy. It can be understood as a kind of relativism in the following way. Karl Marx in proclaiming the advent of communism explicitly avowed atheism. On his analysis the so-called absolute values of the Christian tradition were nothing more than the invention of the propertied classes for the purpose of protecting their property. Teaching people that stealing was immoral was much more effective and economical than posting armed guards. Religion, law, morality, and the state itself were all self-serving tools in the hands of the ruling classes. When Lenin and later Stalin achieved power in Russia they ruled by naked, arbitrary, personal power, sweeping aside all individual rights. God's law was replaced by Stalin's law. Similarly, the Nazis proclaimed that Christianity was a Jewish plot against the Aryan race. All standards of justice were swept aside. Hitler's subjective will became the only law.

From a different perspective totalitarianism looks like a new form of moral absolutism. Communism destroyed the absolute values of Christianity—that is true—but these values were replaced by historical materialism which prescribed equally absolute values. The logic is the same, only the content is different. Stalin did not act arbitrarily; on the contrary, he saw himself as implementing the inexorable laws of history which call for the establishment of the classless society. From the Communist point of view what is wrong with Christian values is only that they are not absolute, that is, they are not true, but Communist values *are* absolute. Along the same lines, for Hitler race was the absolute value. He acted, not arbitrarily, but according to the dictates of the one ultimate truth, Aryan superiority.

It should now be clear that democracy and totalitarianism when examined in terms of theoretical foundations can be understood in two strikingly different ways. The analysis so far presented can be summed up in two propositions. (1) A supporter of democracy who holds that values are relative will see democracy as moral relativism in practice and totalitarianism as moral absolutism in practice. (2) A supporter of democracy who holds that values are absolute will see democracy as moral absolutism in practice and totalitarianism as moral relativism in practice.

The explicit question of the selections contained in this volume is how do Plato's ideas contribute to democracy and totalitarianism. The implicit question is which one of the points of view just mentioned is the correct one. If Plato's arguments are themselves examined, no one, I think, can quarrel with two statements about them. First, Plato did certainly hold that an absolute standard of values exists. Second, Plato's description of the perfect state does in a certain way resemble modern totalitarianism, that is, he provides for a single ruler, he argues that each man has a proper role to play in society, that the well-being of society as a whole is of prime importance, and that each man must be kept in his proper place even against his will. With all of this in mind let us look at the commentaries and the commentators.

In the first section I have included rather substantial selections from the two books which are probably the most important indictments of Plato as a totalitarian: *Plato Today* by R. H. S. Crossman and *The Open Society and Its Enemies* by Karl R. Popper. R. H. S. Crossman, trained as a classical scholar at Oxford, is at present a prominent Labour member of the House of Commons; he has recently been named spokesman for education in the Labour "shadow cabinet." He is a democratic socialist, very much a "majority-rule democrat." *Plato Today* was written in the 1930s when both Hitler and Stalin were at the summit of power. Crossman sees Plato as heavily influenced by authoritarian Sparta, he sees a comparison between the chaotic democracy of the Athens of Plato's time and the Weimar Republic of pre-Hitler Germany. He sees also a comparison between Hitler and Plato's philosopher-king and between the organic Nazi state and Plato's perfect state.

Karl Popper is a scientist and logician. His academic reputation was first made in 1934 with the publication of what has become a classic in the philosophy of science, *Logik der Forschung*, later translated as *The Logic of Scientific Discovery*.

The Open Society and Its Enemies was published in the early 1940s and, as might be expected, is much more explicitly philosophical than Crossman's book. Popper as philosopher of modern science finds Plato's metaphysical doctrines almost wholly erroneous and their political consequences altogether pernicious. For Popper absolute truth cannot be known, but anyone who thinks that he knows

it will inevitably attempt to impose it on everyone else. Plato's absolute truth and his regimented society are in Popper's eyes the very
antithesis of the proper scientific attitude and of democratic government. Popper argues that the only proper intellectual model for
politics is "piecemeal social engineering," that is, the application of
trial and error scientific technique to social problems. This is diametrically opposed to Plato's "utopian social engineering" which
seeks to impose a complete plan on society by the use of force and
"noble fictions" (which for Popper is simply to be translated as "lies"
or "propaganda"). In Popper's view Plato's political program rests
upon his historicist assumption that existing states are decayed forms
of a pre-existing perfect state. Plato's formula, therefore, is establish
the perfect state and then resist all change. Thus, from a logical
point of view Plato's "republic" is identical with modern totalitarianism.

The second section contains selections from John Wild's *Plato's
Modern Enemies and the Theory of Natural Law* and John H. Hallowell's *The Moral Foundation of Democracy*. The central contention here is that Plato's teachings have little to do with modern
totalitarianism; on the contrary, Plato is in reality an intellectual
ancestor of modern democracy. It is important to understand that
there is here no suggestion that Plato was literally a democrat, for,
of course, he was not.

Both Wild and Hallowell share in considerable measure Plato's
philosophical as opposed to his merely political views. They agree
that there are absolute standards of good and justice and that Plato
was largely correct in his account of what these standards are.

Wild writes in direct reply to Crossman, Popper, and others of
similar views. He argues that Plato could not be a supporter of modern democracy for the obvious reason that he knew nothing of
modern democracy. For Plato democracy meant chaotic mob rule.
Plato's contribution to Western civilization is his discovery of sound
standards of right and wrong; his particular political prescriptions are
on the whole bound in time to ancient Greece and are largely incidental to his true importance. Wild opens and Hallowell continues
the theme that Plato was the founder of the idea of natural or higher
law which ultimately comes to fruition in modern democratic government. Plato supported natural law. Modern totalitarianism con-

demns it and substitutes the arbitrary will of the dictator. Thus, far from being similar, they are fundamentally antithetical. Hitler and Stalin were maniacal tyrants; Plato's philosopher-king is by definition a lover and implementor of the good.

Attempting to sum up in a few words the differences between these positions is very difficult, but let me submit the following for the reader's judgment. For Crossman and Popper the prime value is human freedom, a man's opportunity to accept or reject policies or ideas according to his own judgment. Thus, democratic government itself becomes a prime value. Because Plato explicitly rejected democracy in favor of authoritarian rule, Crossman and Popper oppose him. His so-called natural-law doctrine is simply his particular way, just as erroneous as any other absolutism, of rationalizing authoritarian rule. For Wild and Hallowell democratic government is valuable because it has in recent centuries been the repository of natural law. Democracy in this sense is a secondary value; it is only valuable when it implements natural law. So far as Plato is concerned, what is important is that he argued for natural law. That he was not explicitly a political democrat is relatively insignificant.

The final selections are designed to undergird the dispute in sections one and two by examining in greater detail the makeup of Plato's analysis. They serve also as explanations of Plato's philosophical doctrines, particularly the theory of ideas. In "On Classical Political Philosophy" Leo Strauss seeks to show how classical thinkers like Plato and Aristotle themselves looked at political problems. Strauss shows how the attempt was made to replace mere opinion about every-day political matters with firm knowledge concerning right and wrong choices. Strauss argues for the validity of this method and implicitly argues for its acceptance in the modern world.

Bertrand Russell's criticism of Plato's theory of ideas puts this method of replacing opinion with knowledge to the test of modern logic and finds it inadequate. From Russell's point of view Plato's basic philosophical presuppositions are erroneous and, thus, little faith can be put in conclusions derived from them.

The questions which underlie the discussions by Strauss and Russell are: Can absolute values be established and does Plato establish them? Strauss in answering affirmatively supports Wild and Hallowell. Russell in the negative stands with Crossman and Popper.

What has not been done in these introductory remarks is to decide the proper interpretation of Plato or the proper interpretation of totalitarianism and democracy. These questions remain open and because they are important questions the study of Plato and his commentors is important. I have attempted to provide an intellectual framework, to give the reader food for thought. But this is only a beginning. My summaries and generalizations come nowhere near exhausting the richness of Plato's thougnt or of the commentators' discussions. A great many significant and interesting points will arise that I have not touched. Political philosophy is, after all, an almost inexhaustible subject.

I ANCESTOR OF
TOTALITARIANISM

PLATO AND THE PERFECT STATE

R. H. S. Crossman

Plato the man

Socrates' execution was not in vain. By his death, like another conscientious objector four hundred years later, he immortalized the idea which he served; and the legend of Socrates became the inspiration of all who believe in reason. But the man who first formulated the Socratic faith into a systematic philosophy was fundamentally different from his master. Just as Paul of Tarsus created an orthodox Christian theology strangely remote in spirit from that of Jesus, so Plato modified the Socratic ideal of philosophy into a new Platonic system. Plato and Paul were both converts to a faith, but each of them changed the faith of his master almost as much as he was changed by it. And so in the history both of Platonism and of Christianity we find a strange tension between the ideals of the master and of the disciple; and at recurring intervals there is a movement to get behind the disciple's dogma to the real personality of the master. In the end loyalty to both is well-nigh impossible.

Consider for a moment these two men. Plato and Socrates. No two personalities could be more sharply opposed: Socrates, the humorous citizen of Periclean Athens, who knew and loved all sorts and conditions of men; Plato, the aristocrat, who shook the dust of

R. H. S. Crossman *is a Labour Member of Parliament and sometime Fellow of New College, Oxford. "Plato and the Perfect State" is an excerpt from his* Plato Today *(2nd rev.; London: George Allen & Unwin Ltd., 1959). Copyright © 1959 by George Allen & Unwin Ltd. Reprinted by permission of George Allen & Unwin Ltd.*

democratic Athens off his feet: Socrates, the man who knew that he knew nothing; Plato, the systematic exponent of an authoritarian creed; Socrates, the conversationalist, and Plato, the master of prose style: Socrates, the personification of life itself, and Plato, the remote observer of all things living. It will be no surprise to find that the Socratic ideal under Plato's hand has suffered some startling transformations.

However long we study Plato's writings, we can never feel that we know Plato. He baffles and eludes our search, and although we may learn a good deal *about* him, to know or to like him as a man is almost impossible. This is due not only to his deliberate self-effacement in the dialogues—in his letters we possess extremely personal expressions of opinion—but also to his character. Plato was a divided personality, a man who deliberately denied himself full realization; a poet who deliberately allowed the springs of imagination to dry up. Unless we remember this we shall not grasp the full tragedy of his life. For he was first and foremost an artist, to whom practical affairs were of small interest. His poems are among the most exquisite we possess—and yet the story may well be true that the young Plato burned his tragedies and devoted himself to the cause of philosophy and of the regeneration of Greece. This decision was forced upon him by three things: his social position as a member of the ruling class who was naturally expected to devote his life to public service, the death of Socrates, which compelled him to see the urgency of the crisis, and lastly, the experiences of his youth.

Plato was born in 428 B.C. Pericles was dead: the great plague had ravaged Athens and the dreary years of the Peloponnesian war had just begun. Athens, connected by the Long Walls to her port, the Piraeus, had become an armed camp into which each summer were huddled the Attic farmers, sheltering from the Spartan invasion and watching their crops burnt. Plato as a boy can have known little save war and the rumors of war, revolution and the rumors of revolution. War is never healthy for democracies, and as Plato grew up, Athens began to crack under the strain. As money ran short and the standard of living fell, the democratic leaders became more and more imperialist. In 430 Athens had been fighting to defend her Empire: by 416 it was necessary not only to repel attacks, but to recoup the losses of the war by some material gains—and Athens launched out on the enterprise of conquering Sicily, the richest island of the Mediterranean. The failure of the Sicilian expedition—caused in part by the defection of Socrates' favorite pupil, Alcibiades—meant the downfall of Athens, and in 404, she capitulated. Defeat in war brought revolution at home and an aristocratic terror was established. Plato was just twenty-four when this happened.

Belonging to one of the most distinguished families in all Athens, he had been brought up in an atmosphere of counter-revolution. In aristocratic circles, by this time, democracy was only another name for corruption and class-politics, and it was taken as self-evident that nothing but armed revolution could save her from collapse. Plato had never seen Periclean Athens: instead, he had heard the savage jeers of the wealthy nobles at the inefficiency and vulgarity of the jingo democrats, and felt their growing terror of the uneducated proletariat with whom sovereignty lay. As the situation became worse, the cry for leadership grew louder, and at last the people itself began to tire of its freedom. The aristocratic politicians saw their opportunity, and Plato believed that the turning-point had now come; his friends would initiate the rule of Law and Order. Long afterwards, in a letter, he described his feelings in those troubled days:

> My experience as a young man was by no means unusual. I thought that as soon as I became my own master I would immediately enter public life. A sudden change, however, in the political situation diverted me from my plan. The democratic regime of the time was generally detested and a revolution took place. It was headed by fifty-one leaders, of whom eleven were in the City and ten in the Piraeus: these two committees dealt with the market and with the administration of the two towns. Above them was a supreme committee of thirty. Some of the members of this supreme committee were relations or acquaintances of mine and invited me to join them, imagining that I should find the new regime to my taste. My feelings were in no way surprising if you consider my age at the time. I thought the new regime would substitute the reign of justice for the reign of injustice, and so I gave it my closest attention to see what it would do. And I saw these gentlemen within a very short time make the democracy they had destroyed seem like a golden age! They actually ordered my aged friend Socrates, whom I would not hesitate to call the most upright man of his time,

to take part in the arrest of a citizen whom they wished to put out of the way. Their intention was to associate Socrates, whether he wished it or no, with the activities of the new regime. He refused to obey and was prepared to face death rather than be made an accessory to their crimes.

When I saw all this and a good deal else besides I was deeply disgusted and dissociated myself entirely from this deplorable government. Shortly afterwards, the thirty were turned out and their whole regime destroyed. Once again I was really, though less urgently, filled with a desire to take an active part in politics. Athens was still very unsettled and revolting incidents were not uncommon. It was not surprising that those revolutionary times resulted in personal reprisals of a violent character: but on the whole the restored democracy exercised considerable moderation. And yet, as ill-luck would have it, certain influential persons brought an action against Socrates. The charge was an outrageous one, of which Socrates was completely innocent. They accused him of impiety, and on this count the jury condemned to death the man who previously, when some of them had the misfortune to be in exile themselves, had refused to take part in the arrest of one of their own friends.

When I considered all this, the type of men who were administering affairs, and the condition of the Law and of public morality—the more I considered it and the older I grew, the more difficult appeared to me the task of decent government. It was impossible to take action without friends or political associates, and these it was not easy to find among the politicians, since their methods of government were false to the true principles and traditional institutions of our country. To find new men for the job, however, was an impossibility. Moreover, statutes and usages alike were degenerating in Athens with surprising rapidity, and so, although at first I was filled with an ardent desire to enter politics, when I considered all this and saw how chaotic the political situation was, I felt completely baffled. I continued to consider how on earth some improvement could be brought about, not only in the administration, but also in society as a whole, and I was constantly on the lookout for an opportunity to intervene. But finally I came to the conclusion that every city without exception is badly governed, and that the state of legislation is everywhere so deplorable that no government is possible without drastic reconstruction combined with some very good luck. And so I was forced to extol true philosophy and to declare that through it alone can real justice both for the State and for the individual be discovered and enforced. Mankind (I said) will find no cessation from evil until either the real philosophers gain political control or else the politicians become by some miracle real philosophers.[1]

It is clear from this quotation that the shortcomings of the antidemocratic revolution were the first great disappointment of Plato's life: they shook him out of his complacency and made him reconsider his whole position. Up till now he had assumed that everything could be put right only if the gentlemen gained control. Now he realized that "gentlemen" could behave worse than the demagogues of the proletariat. But this did not alter his profound contempt for the working population. Plato remained an aristocrat, convinced that the peasant, the craftsman, and the shopkeeper were incapable of political responsibility. Government was the perquisite of the gentry, who did not need to earn a living and could therefore devote their lives to the responsibilities of war and politics. In the eyes of the young Plato there must always be a ruling aristocracy and a subject people. The latter were the producers and distributors of material wealth, and Plato had a special word, *banausic*, to express his contempt for their menial occupations. The former had the paternal care of the state at heart. Living on the labor of the subject masses, they gave them in return security, justice, and defense. Because they were of a nobler breed, culture and education belonged to them, while to the subjects was allotted that technical training which would best increase their efficiency as craftsmen or farmers. The political philosophy of the young Plato was at bottom a longing to return to the Homeric age of chivalry. Drawn from his reading of the *Iliad*, it postulated a radical reconstruction of the social order. The working classes must be put in their place: the gentry must regain their old self-confidence and sense of responsibility.

The failure of the antidemocratic revolution did not profoundly alter Plato's view: it merely proved that the reconstruction could not come through the normal political channels. A discredited aristocracy could never win power at Athens: but this did not prove that aristoc-

[1] See Plato, Letter VII.

racy as such was wrong. Somehow, on Plato's view, the gentry must be trained to play their proper part. How that was to be done he did not know, and was content for the moment to devote himself to mathematics and pure philosophy, and to discussions with Socrates, his master and friend.

Then came the trial and the death of Socrates. It is noteworthy that Plato did not lay it to the charge of the restored democracy, but admitted that the new government acted with considerable moderation. He saw, indeed, that it was one of those events which no foresight or human volition could have prevented. But because it could happen under a moderate democracy, it disturbed him profoundly. For years he had talked with Socrates and studied with him the new science and mathematics and theology: more than most of his contemporaries he had understood the Socratic spirit. He had not failed to see Socrates' deep disgust with the aristocratic clique and his contempt for their *Realpolitik*. He had grasped the reason for his refusal to escape from prison, and seen him as he was, not an agnostic, but a conscientious objector. Now that he was dead, Plato felt himself alone, but he also felt that his vocation was clear. He must overcome his deep revulsion from politics and do what Socrates had failed to do. He must answer the questions which Socrates asked, and discover those eternal principles of human conduct which alone could bring happiness to the individual and stability to the State. He must use the Socratic dialectic not only to discredit hypocrisy and false pretensions, but to reveal what real justice and courage and temperance are, and then work out a constitution and a system of law consistent with them. And lastly, he must build a city-state so firmly based upon reason and truth that Socrates, the conscientious objector, could have given it his wholehearted approval and loyalty, and lived with a good conscience under its protection. For Socrates' death, he believed, could only be made good if it inspired his friends and disciples to devote themselves to this one task.

Throughout his life Plato regarded himself as the fulfilment of Socrates. Because he believed this, he wrote Dialogues and made no attempt to show where Socrates speaks in his own name and where he is the mouthpiece of Plato. Any such distinction would have seemed unreal to the man who had grasped the meaning of Socrates' life. Reason and truth are not the trappings of individual personalities: they are eternal and universal, and in them individual differences disappear. So at least both Plato and Socrates believed, and therefore the distinction of the real from the Platonic Socrates was for Plato absurd. Devotion to his memory would encourage Plato to a meticulous recreation of the world in which Socrates lived and talked, but not to a rigid separation of the master's philosophy from his own.

In his written works Plato tried to give flesh and blood to the Socratic spirit, the spirit of philosophy. The Dialogues are not dogmatic assertions of truth, but examples of philosophy at work, exposing falsehood, asserting new principles, finding fault again with these new principles and ascending ever higher in search of laws completely acceptable to reason. For Plato, the dialogue was the proper medium of philosophical thought because it displayed in its very form the fact that truth can only be found by *cooperation*; and—up to the time when he wrote the *Republic*—the Socratic dialogues were his only published work because Socrates was for him the supreme embodiment of this method.

It is impossible in one short chapter to solve a problem argued by scholars for hundreds of years. The relation of Plato to Socrates is a problem of this sort but it is doubtful whether much of the argument has been of profit. Plato was no Boswell devoted to the immortalization of a Johnson far greater than himself. On the other hand his Socrates was not a fiction behind which his own personality was screened. If we look for analogies, we shall find one not in the writer of the Fourth Gospel, but in St. Paul. The Fourth Gospel is the work of a contemplative and placid mind. The Dialogues are as fiercely controversial and pugnaciously loyal as Paul's epistles. Both writers feel themselves so immersed in the mission of the men whom they describe that it is difficult to separate what was original from the added touches. Socrates was an individual whom Plato had loved and whose memory he wished to perpetuate, but he was also the founder of a movement far greater than himself, which Plato believed himself to have developed upon true Socratic lines, but far beyond the point which Socrates had reached. For this reason the Socrates of the Dialogues is at the same time the historical Socrates and the timeless spokesman of Platonic philosophy. Plato saw no inconsistency in this.

But writing was not enough. Socrates had demanded not only the discovery of truth, but its embodiment in human society: the double demand must be fulfilled, and Plato decided to prepare himself for the task. He could not now renounce politics and find consolation in poetry or in pure philosophy, although every natural inclination urged him to do so. Science and mathematics must, if Socrates were right, be harnessed in the cause of Greek regeneration: they must not be allowed to become a way of escape for an *intelligentsia* grown weary and anxious to avoid its civic responsibilities. Plato must have been greatly tempted by the claims of pure speculation. It was as easy for him as for the modern academic to pretend that truth alone was his objective, and that its applicability in the real world was not and should not be the concern of the pure scientist or philosopher: that theory and practice were rightly divorced from one another and that the former should be proud of its remoteness from everyday life.

There are many passages in the Dialogues in which Plato expresses his distaste for practical life[2] and extols the virtues of academic research. But always on such occasions an element of self-justification is apparent. The well-born recluse tries to rationalize his hatred of the mob into a theory of human stupidity. The academic, distrusting his political capacities, demonstrates the triviality of politics. But the apologia is always uneasy. Plato could never devote himself to metaphysics without feeling the prick of conscience reminding him that metaphysics were an escape from life. In the *Republic* (496) he says:

> There is only a handful left who are inspired by the true spirit of philosophy, among them perhaps a man of noble character who was brought up in a good home and was saved from corrupting influences by banishment, and so has remained true to his own nature: or a great personality born in a small city who despises the petty politics of his home town and can therefore see beyond them.
>
> Those who become members of this small company and have made philosophy their own realize the pleasures and the blessedness which it brings and appreciate fully the madness which has taken possession of the masses. They all know that to all intents and purposes nothing sound is ever achieved by the politicians, and that no one who tries to uphold justice will find any support on which he can rely. He will indeed be like a man who has fallen

[2] See particularly the *Phaedo* and the *Theaetetus* (172).

into a den of beasts, refusing to accept the law of the jungle but unable by himself to hold out against a bestial world: and so, before he can do anything for the city or his friends, he is put away, and a life is wasted without profit to himself or anyone else.

Considering all this coolly and objectively, the philosopher will remain quietly at his own work like a traveller caught in a storm who retreats behind a wall to shelter from the driving gusts of dust and hail. Seeing the rest of the world filled full with iniquity, he will be content to keep his own life here on earth unstained by wickedness and impious actions, so that he may leave this world with a fair hope of the next, at peace with himself and God.

This streak in Plato's character is never wholly absent from his writings. It accounts for his ignorance of human nature—the natural superior can rarely understand the mob which he despises—and also for the uncertainty which runs through his whole career as to the purpose and direction of his researches and teaching. Later moralists and philosophers have shown the same defect—an inclination to forestall criticism of practical failure by saying in advance, "I'm willing to try my hand at putting the world to rights: but if my suggestions fail, I take no responsibility since my real interest is in pure theory."

It was the influence of Socrates which saved Plato from renouncing practical life. Socrates may have had a remote and mystical religion, but his intense interest in the world around him made it ridiculous even to suggest that he could take refuge in pure speculation. The fact that Socrates' feelings for Athens and his enjoyment of the life of the busy city had never wavered even in the face of death, was a constant reminder to Plato that a great teacher must also be a simple human being who loves and understands his fellow men. Plato could never be that, but at least he could apply the knowledge which he gained to the discovery of some cure for the miseries of his fellow men.

With these intentions, shortly after Socrates' death, he left Athens and traveled for several years in the Mediterranean, probably visiting, among other places, North Africa, Egypt, and Sicily. He himself has recorded for us the impression which the first sight of the court of Dionysius I, Tyrant of Syracuse, produced upon him.

I was by no means content with the "blissful life" which I found there, consisting, as it did, of incessant debauches. No one whose life is spent on gorging food twice a day and sharing his bed at night, and so on, could ever attain real wisdom. The human constitution cannot stand the strain of that sort of life for long. Nor would he ever be likely to learn self-control or any other virtue. What is more, no State, however good its laws, can retain any stability if its citizens believe in mad extravagance and exert themselves only in the activities of eating and drinking and in the vigorous pursuit of their amours. Inevitably in such a state there is a constant succession of tyrannies, oligarchies, and democracies; and politicians cannot endure the mention of just government or equality before the law.

This visit to Sicily and South Italy was to prove of great importance in Plato's development. In the first place he became acquainted with Archytas, the geometer, who was trying to apply Pythagorean principles to the government of his native city Tarentum. Here Plato could see realized in a wealthy Italian town his dream of the rule of reason, and the sight must have encouraged him in his own designs. In the second place, in Syracuse, he met Dion, the son-in-law of Dionysius I, and immediately struck up a close friendship with him. A statesman of great practical ability, Dion was for Plato the ideal man of action. A passionate student of philosophy, he was willing to submit himself to the Platonic discipline and was later to become an ardent pupil in the Academy. But, above all, he was the *friend* of Plato; the two seemed to be complementary to each other, the politician with a bent for philosophy and the philosopher driven by his conscience into the practical world. After Socrates, Dion was the most important influence in Plato's life.

At the age of forty Plato returned to Athens to see in 387 the conclusion of the ignominious peace of Antalcidas by which all Asia Minor was surrendered to Persia. Hellenic independence was ebbing, but the old feud between Sparta and Athens still continued and Athens had won back something of the glories of the empire from her rival. Plato, however, had made his decision. Athens offered him no prospects and so in a shady garden outside the walls he founded his new university—the Academy.

The Academy was both a school and an institute of scientific research. There, for the first time, the two sides of modern university life were joined together. Visited by nearly all the famous scientists of the time, it soon ceased to be an Athenian institution and became one of the centers of Greek learning. The students, too, were by no means exclusively from Athens, but included the sons (and daughters!) of some of the most distinguished families in Greece. Plato renounced Athenian politics to become the president of the first pan-Hellenic university. In a later chapter [not included here] we shall see something of the educational system which he proceeded to build up: at present we are concerned to observe only the double purpose of the Academy, on the one side as an organization for pure research, and on the other as a training ground for young men of the leisured classes (and mostly of noble blood) who were destined to a political career in their home cities. Here, at last, Plato had found a field for practical activity which was not confined to Athenian party-politics: here he could build up a community of young disciples and imbue them with the moral and intellectual discipline which was necessary if they were to restore the ancient glories of Greece. In the pure air of the Academy they could throw off party and factional interests and avoid the corruption of life in the degenerate city-state. Steeped in the spirit of philosophy, they would become leaders of a new and purer Hellenism and carry back with them to their homes the revolutionary creed of the Academy.

For twenty years Plato was content to guide the policy of the new university, and in a series of Socratic dialogues to indicate the lines along which its research should be conducted. But in 367, when he was close on sixty, an event happened in Sicily which was to provide the philosopher with a test of the practical utility of his work. Dionysius I of Syracuse died and was succeeded by his son, Dionysius II. The latter, a young man of thirty, was not a strong character and his education, or lack of it, had done little to improve his natural capacities. For this reason Dion became the power behind the throne and suggested to the new tyrant that Plato should be invited to undertake his education and to advise him on general policy. The invitation was given and Plato set sail for Sicily.

We need not carry the story of Plato's life further,[3] for it is the Plato of 367 B.C. whom we have decided to confront with the problems of our modern world. It is clearly impossible to ask what Plato would think today without specifying more precisely which Plato we mean, the young disillusioned politician, the middle-aged president of the Academy, serenely certain of the power of philosophy to rule the world, or the old man, sceptical and cautious, who composed the *Laws*. It is the second of these whom we have chosen, and for this reason we shall take as representative of his thought the famous dialogue called the *Republic*, which he composed some years before his journey to Sicily. The *Republic* was not only the manifesto of the Academy, but also the program of the philosopher statesman, and if we read it carefully, we can observe many indications that it was composed with the possibility of an invitation from Syracuse constantly in view. It has, therefore, a peculiar appropriateness to our present task, since it discusses all the main philosophical problems, with reference to practical political questions.

Plato's program of political reform

The *Republic* contains Plato's plan for the building of a perfect state in which every citizen is really happy. He imagines himself invested with supreme power and asks how he would use it to save humanity from its present miseries. But if you are going to build a perfect society, you can only do so by reconstructing existing institutions; and so Plato was forced to consider the city which he knew so well, and to ask himself what was wrong with Athens. When he had discovered this, he could construct a city free from the evils of Athenian society.

Plato believed that these evils were three in number: class war, bad government, and bad education. Class war was the most obvious of the three. Most Greek cities were either oligarchies or democracies and many alternated through a series of revolutions between these two forms of class dictatorship. In the former political power was held by an alliance of landowners and merchants with the support of the farmers and peasants: in the latter the leaders of the town proletariat molded policy with the uneasy support of certain commer-

---

[3] For some account of Plato's later life see Chapter 10 [of Crossman's book].

cial interests. In both the opposition was ruthlessly fleeced. The effect of the Peloponnesian war had been to intensify the political struggle. It has been described by Thucydides in a famous passage.[4]

> The whole Greek world was convulsed by the great war. In each city the democratic politicians called on Athens to assist them in their domestic conflict, while the oligarchs relied on Sparta. In peace time they would have had no justification and no desire for foreign intervention; but in war the weapon of alliance was ready to hand. Each side could use it for its own benefit and for the destruction of its opponents, and intervention could be employed by anyone who was plotting a *putsch*. Revolution brought those horrors to the cities of Greece which will always recur so long as human nature is unchanged, and which vary in their intensity and character according to the variations of the social conditions. In peace time and in prosperity state and individual alike are actuated by higher motives, because they are not faced with inevitable choices. But war destroys the comfortable routine of life, schools us in violence, and adapts our character to the new conditions. . . . The cause of all these evils was imperialism, whose fundamental motives are ambition and the acquisitive instinct, and from which arises the fanaticism of class conflict. The politicians on each side were equipped with high-sounding slogans: the Left claimed that they were the champions of the constitutional rights of the people, the Right that they stood for aristocracy, law, and order. Both boasted that they were devoted servants of the community and both made the community the prize of war. The only purpose of their policy was the extermination of their opponents, and to achieve this they flinched from nothing. Even worse were the reprisals which they perpetrated in total disregard of morality or of the common good. The only standard which they recognized was party caprice, and so they were prepared, either by the perversion of justice or by revolutionary action, to glut the passing passions engendered by the struggle. Religion was respected by neither: they preferred to applaud the use of fair phrases for the achievement of odious ends. Between them the middle class was wiped out, either because they refused to participate or because neither side could bear to let them survive.
>
> Thus class-conflict produced every form of evil in the Greek

[4] *Thucydides*, III, 82.

world. Simplicity, which is an essential element in true nobility of character, was ridiculed and disappeared. Society was divided into warring camps, suspicious of one another. Where no contract or obligation was binding, nothing could heal the conflict, and since security was only to be found in the assumption that nothing was secure, everyone took steps to preserve himself and no one could afford to trust his neighbor. On the whole the baser types survived best. Aware of their own deficiencies and their opponents' abilities, they resorted boldly to violence, before they were defeated in debate and struck down by a conspiracy of minds more versatile than their own; whereas the more intelligent, confident that they could anticipate the others' plans and that it was unnecessary to use crude methods where subtle policy was possible, were taken off their guard and so destroyed.

To the modern mind, attuned to the concept of indirect aggression, Thucydides' analysis needs no explanation. In his day, as in ours, the clash of ideologies could only too easily destroy the possibility of peaceful change and constitutional government. Wherever that occurred, violence became the only weapon in the struggle for survival, and dictatorship the only organization to ensure economic interests. Plato realized that, unless the class war could be ended, Greek culture could not long survive. But between the Left and the Right he, like Thucydides, found little to choose. Both were actuated by selfish class interests: both were willing to sacrifice the national welfare to the immediate interests of their supporters. Both used religion and morality as rhetorical devices for attaining their material ends. If there were any advantage, it lay with the oligarchs, for their system was more stable: because policy was concentrated in the hands of a few, it was less likely to be swayed by gusts of popular passion. On Plato's view the class war, if it were allowed to continue, could end logically only in the destruction of all social life. For the qualities necessary to survival were not decency or wisdom or righteousness, but brutality and low cunning.

But if the class war was the prime evil of Athenian life, there were, in Plato's opinion, two other contributory evils of great importance. The first was the idea that government belonged by right to a particular social class *or* to the people as a whole. He believed that it was a whole-time job and demanded abilities of a peculiar kind. The State could only prosper if political power were granted to men and women who were capable of using it correctly. But the oligarchs regarded government as the perquisite of wealth, the democrats of citizenship, and so under both parties the government was selected for reasons which had little to do with its capacity for ruling. The result was that in each case the machinery of State became the instrument of class interest: law did not rule but was enslaved to a section of its own subjects. It was on this score that Plato leveled his most bitter attacks against Athenian democracy. The people claimed to govern themselves and proudly refused to submit the control of policy to any body of experts. Instead the citizen assembly itself made all important decisions. And what was the result? The people being incompetent, power fell into the hands of demagogues: and "ruling" became the perquisite not of the wise statesman, but of the mob-orator who knew how to cajole the people and to pander to its worst tastes.

Conceive something of this kind happening on board ship, on one ship or on several. The master is bigger and stronger than all the crew, but rather deaf and short-sighted. His seamanship is as deficient as his hearing. The sailors are quarrelling about the navigation. Each man thinks that he ought to navigate, though up to that time he has never studied the art, and cannot name his instructor or the time of his apprenticeship. They go further and say that navigation cannot be taught, and are ready to cut in pieces him who says that it can. They crowd round the solitary master, entreating him and offering him every inducement to entrust them with the helm. Occasionally when they fail to persuade him and others succeed, they kill those others and throw them overboard, overpower the noble master by mandragora or drink or in some other way, and bind him hand and foot. Then they rule the ship and make free with the cargo, and so drinking and feasting make just such a voyage as might be expected of men like them. Further, they compliment anyone who has the skill to contrive how they may persuade or compel the master to set them over the ship, and call him a good seaman, a navigator, and a master of seamanship; any other kind of man they despise as useless. They have no notion that the true navigator must attend to the year and the seasons, to the sky and the stars and the winds, and all that concerns his craft, if he is really going to be fit to rule a ship. They do not believe that it is possible for anyone to acquire by skill or practice the art of getting control of the helm, whether there is opposition or not, and at the same time to master the art of steering. If ships were managed in that way, do you not think that the true navigator would certainly be called a star gazer and a useless babbler by the crews of ships of that description? [5]

This was Plato's picture of Athenian democracy—a poor old skipper bullied, deceived, and cajoled by a gang of knaves; and he believed that its desperate plight was caused by its refusal to admit that law and order are only possible if government is in the hands of an elite specially trained for the task.

From this follows naturally his third criticism of Athens. Education, which should be the major responsibility of the State, had been left to individual caprice and to the individual's capacity to pay. Here again was a task which should be entrusted only to the expert and to the man of proven probity. The future of any State depends on the younger generation, and it is therefore madness to allow the minds of children to be molded by individual taste and force of circumstance. Equally disastrous had been the State's laissez-faire policy with regard to teachers and schoolmasters and sophist-lecturers. It had allowed anyone who wished to earn his living in this way, whatever he taught. As a result the man in the street, under the influence of irresponsible publicists, demagogues, and rhetoricians, had ceased to believe that such things as law or justice existed. The equalitarian philosophy which held that each man's opinion was as good as his neighbor's had destroyed respect for authority and had turned democracy into licentious anarchy. Disregard of education was primarily responsible for this.

Faced by these three cardinal errors of Athenian democracy, Plato turned naturally enough—for he was an aristocrat—to Sparta. Here was a State which—apart from occasional serf revolutions—had maintained its social and political stability for 200 years. Sparta had not avoided the class war, but she had coped with it so successfully that she had escaped revolution. Plato saw that there were three reasons for this. In the first place, Sparta's economy was self-sufficient: she was an agricultural State with no imperial pretensions. In the second

[5] *Republic*, 488, Lindsay's translation.

place, government there was in the hands of a specially trained hereditary ruling caste to whom the pleasures of wealth and luxury were forbidden; and lastly, in Sparta education was rigidly controlled by the State. Sparta had avoided all the evils of Athenian democracy, and Plato could not but admire her laconic austerity and her aristocratic contempt for commerce and self-government. His ideal State was to be framed on a Spartan model.

But his own political experience had shown him that Sparta was not the perfect State. To begin with, the ruthless suppression of serfs and the constant fear of revolution which accompanied it could not satisfy the idealist who wished to make every citizen happy. Plato dreamed of a civilized Sparta in which the serfs would be subjects, voluntarily submitting to the rule of law, not slaves terrorized by a secret police. But further, the Spartan ruling class had in his own lifetime demonstrated its own limitations. After 404 Sparta had succeeded to the Athenian Empire, and Spartan citizens had been sent out to administrate many of the towns once ruled by Athens. The results had been disastrous. Soldiers who had been used to barrack discipline and whose natural desires had been suppressed by rigid social tabus, found themselves in positions of irresponsible authority where they could do whatever they liked without let or hindrance. Alone on his island, the Spartan administrator suddenly discovered a new world of pleasures, and a new delight in giving, not receiving, commands. Like the public (private) schoolboy in his first term at the university, he "let himself go," and within a few years the Spartan Empire was infamous for the cruelty and corruption of its administration. Once the individual was allowed to make money and enjoy the pleasures of self-expression, he discarded his aristocratic sobriety and military restraint and became a vulgar and brutal voluptuary: once the State discovered the pleasures of imperialism, it accepted them without any of its responsibilities.

Plato had seen this happen, and had realized that the cure for Athens was not simply a dose of Spartan tonic. Something else must be added, and he believed that this "something else" was to be found in the Academy.

For the Academy was designed to produce that spirit of disinterested research of which Socrates had been a living example. Its students were to become statesmen, who voluntarily submitted to the law of reason because they saw that this law was true and right. The Spartan boy had been taught the soldier's unreasoning submission to the commands of his superior. He had been "socially conditioned" to obey law, and for this reason, when he had to act on his own initiative and had no superior officer to control him, he could offer no resistance to natural desire. Just as "public school morality" often breaks down when the public schoolboy is isolated from his social class and can indulge himself in a whole gamut of forbidden pleasures without fear of disapproval, so Spartan militarism had failed to resist the temptations of imperial power. The Academy, however, provided just the university training which is supposed to turn a conventional public school morality into a reasoned and intellectual self-discipline: its products were not to be mere creatures of habit, but adult men with wills of their own, who understood the principles of law and decided voluntarily to obey them.

Thus while Sparta provided the foundations of the Platonic State, the Academy was to turn it from a tyranny into a benevolent dictatorship, which would rely not on sheer force, but on impartial government to retain the obedience of the subject class. The public schoolboy must be put under the command of the university graduate, his conventional morality controlled by the law of reason.

In the *Republic* Plato sketches the plan of a three-class State. At the top are the *philosopher-kings*; then come the *administrators*, and below them both are all the *civilians*, who are not fit to rule themselves.[6]

---

[6] The words Plato used to describe his three classes are φιλοσοφοι (philosophers), επιχουροι (auxiliaries), and δημιουργοι (craftsmen), but the literal translations of the two latter are so misleading that I have avoided them in the text. Since Plato's lowest class includes all the population except the ruling elite, "working-classes" is as misleading a translation as "craftsmen," and I have finally decided on the word "civilian" to indicate the passive unpolitical nature of the third class. Plato's rulers are also soldiers, so that the word is not wholly amiss so long as it is clearly understood that its meaning is not exhausted in this contrast of soldier and civilian but must include also the contrast of "politically responsible" and "politically subject."

The substitution of "administrator" for "auxiliary" needs less defense. "Auxiliary" to the modern ear means precisely nothing: administrator at least gives something of the prime ideas of "active management" and "public service," and indicates the difference between the second class who are executive—at once the army and the civil service of the new State—and the first who are purely deliberative. Below these two, and carefully segregated from them, are the civilian masses,

And so we reach the famous proposition in which Plato summarized his whole political program. "The city-state can only be saved if the kings become philosophers or the philosophers become kings." Plato was convinced (as Socrates had been) that the good State is the rational State, and that the good ruler is the man who knows precisely the plan of life which will give men happiness. The ruler must understand the world he lives in, and the laws which control it. He must know the science of politics as clearly as the craftsman knows his special skill. Ruling is not everybody's job. It is as specialized as any other science or craft. We do not imagine that *anyone* can attend us when we are ill, nor do we elect our doctors democratically. We demand knowledge and experience of them, and we submit ourselves obediently to their commands. If we did not we should suffer in health. Plato held that the same was true of politics. The ruler must be as highly trained as a doctor and he must be obeyed as implicitly as we obey our doctor's orders.

But the doctor looks after only our bodily health and he attends us only when we are ill. The ruler is always with us: he must direct our whole lives, plan our existence, and order our thoughts and emotions as well as our bodies. Because he controls our whole lives, his training must be more arduous and his knowledge far wider than that of the doctor. The ruler (in Plato's language, the philosopher-king) must know the whole good for man and he must have the character and resolution to impose it upon us without stint. He must not be beguiled by our complaints or tempted by our bribes. He must care about the plan which he knows to be our salvation so much that he can overlook the distress and pain which we shall suffer, just as the doctor must neglect our suffering if he is to save our life. In politics there are no anesthetics or drugs to make the suffering easier for the patient to bear. For the good of the State the ruler must punish and banish and kill the citizen who objects to the political operation the State must undergo.

Thus the three-class State is really a two-class State with a subdivision in the ruling class. The civilians are the vast majority of the population, the peasants and artisans and tradesmen who are engaged

whose only civic duty is obedience to law, and abstention from all political activity. The Greek city-state is to be regenerated by Spartan discipline under the direction of the philosophic spirit of the Academy.

in the production and distribution of wealth. Their function is to provide the material basis of social welfare, their happiness to enjoy the just fruits of their labors under the stable regime of law and order. Plato wastes little time in discussing their organization, but he assumes that his city will be economically self-sufficient and will not depend on imports for the necessities of life. Self-sufficiency will avoid the need for imperialism and for the navy which[7] had given political power in Athens to the urban worker. In his city there will be no town-proletariat or big-business or international bankers to upset the natural harmony of economic interest. And so he need not worry about the civilians since the economic system will run itself provided that political power is forbidden to the producer and distributor of wealth. Class-conflict arose through the control of government by one vested interest: it is removed, according to Plato, by allowing no vested interest whatsoever to influence the government. By depriving every economic interest of the means of opposition, he is confident that he can restore the natural identity of interest, create the possibility of an impartial State, and so remove the possibility of oppression.

For once he has destroyed the power of the vested interests, a real aristocracy or *dictatorship of the best* is possible. From earliest childhood the ruling class is segregated from the civilians, and given a special education. They are to be gentlemen, unsullied by trade and the menial labors of agriculture and craftsmanship: and they are to follow the gentleman's calling of public service in the administration and the army. Whereas the civilian, with his vulgar interests in his craft, in money-making and in family-life, is a natural subject, the ruler, conscious of the social responsibility which higher intellectual and moral capacities bring, is a natural gentleman; and in Plato's State only the gentleman must rule. As children, these natural gentlemen are subjected to an iron discipline. Their fairy stories, their songs, and their dances—all the influences which can mold their character —are censored and controlled. For they are to be the defenders of the State against internal discord and foreign aggression and on their absolute integrity depends the well-being of the whole community. Their education, therefore, is chiefly concerned to ensure three things. In the first place all personal interests must be suppressed, the desire

[7] See page 27 [of Crossman's book].

for wealth, family, bodily pleasures, and so on. For such interests, if they become paramount in a ruler's life, will corrupt his administration and make him another wage-earner no better than the civilians. Plato's elite, therefore, must be given a moral training so strict and so severe that nothing can divert them from their service to the State. Secondly, they must be physically fit, and so they are brought up to a Spartan simplicity of diet and dress. For they are to be soldiers as well as administrators and they must be inured to military discipline from earliest childhood. Lastly, they must be given the rudiments of mental discipline. But their real intellectual education starts only at the age of twenty. Then they must concentrate for ten years upon higher mathematics and dialectic, until at thirty an examination is held in which future philosophers are selected.

Those who fail to pass this examination are the administrators proper, and it is their task to carry out the commands of the philosopher-kings. Unable themselves to become philosophers, they see that only obedience to philosophy will bring peace and security to men. Essentially men of action, ambitious for themselves and for the city, they have outgrown the petty pleasures of private life and find in public service their supreme happiness. Though they cannot themselves think creatively, they can apply the principles of philosophy once they are laid down, and their moral training has been such that nothing can divert them from this purpose.

The philosophers and the administrators live in barracks apart from the civilians. All military and civil power is in their hands, but they receive only a scanty wage from the subject population, and they are absolutely forbidden to have any contact with wealth. Owning nothing, they must guard the property of others, and they will do this faithfully only if their education has taught them to care for higher things. If a man wants wealth, he is not denied the fulfilment of his desire, but he must forfeit political power. Conversely, if he wants a life of public service, he is given the opportunity, provided that he renounces all interest in property. For it is only, on Plato's view, by the complete separation of political power from ownership of property that class war can be abolished and the profit motive become the servant, not the tyrant, of society.

Plato believed that in a State reconstructed upon these lines, the happiness of every individual could be secured. Sacrifices are demanded from each class, but only to ensure the satisfaction of its dominant interest. By the surrender of political freedom, which has brought him only class war, the civilian gains a stable regime in which rulers of absolute integrity will dispense justice, and well-trained soldiers will defend him from attack. He has lost his civil liberties, too, but he has no need of them, now that the social order is really just and impartial. For criticism is only necessary where rulers are corrupt: and the civilian is not the man to criticize since he has neither the knowledge nor the training to do so. The sacrifice of civil liberties, therefore, is the sacrifice of something which he was incapable of doing well and undertook only under the pressure of necessity. Apart from these losses—which many in Europe bear today with equanimity even when they are not blessed with the rule of philosopher-kings—his gains are enormous: in the first place, justice which is impossible under any other regime; in the second place, a certainty that his property will remain his own and that no one will take it from him. Plato believed that few men would ask for more.

The administrators will be happy too. Since their dominant interest is in government, and the driving motive of their life is ambition, they cannot but be content to hold in their hands the executive power of the State. After their early training they will not greatly miss the wealth which they must forgo, or even be upset by the law which forbids them to marry and have families;[8] for they are soldiers, inured to barrack life and to the sacrifice of personal pleasures for the sake of the common weal. As soldiers, too, they will be content on all decisive questions to obey the commands of the philosopher-kings—they know that they themselves do not know. Lastly, the philosophers will be happy, although they have the heaviest sacrifice to make. For their paramount interest is in research and yet they are compelled to spend much time and labor applying the results of their researches to the practical affairs of State. Plato had a natural sympathy with the few who could appreciate the life of "a scholar and a gentleman" and yet were forced to enter the political arena, and among British statesmen would have recognized in A. J. Balfour the characteristics of a true philosopher-king. It was men of this type alone that he chose for supreme political responsibility, hoping that a select band of Balfours would be able to relieve each other in rotation

[8] See Chapter 7 [of Crossman's book].

of the practical work for which they would all feel a justifiable distaste.

Such in barest outline was Plato's program for the salvation of Greece—the restoration of the impartial rule of law through the dictatorship of the philosopher-kings. Only thus could the three evils of class war, bad government, and bad education be cured and happiness provided for every citizen. The Academy must become not only the conscience but the political dictator of Greek society. In every city a Platonic scholar must be vested with absolute power.

There is no doubt that Plato faced the inevitability of the use of force for the achievement of these ends. His statesmen were to be trained soldiers with armies at their disposal, ready if necessary to meet force with force. But he believed that the extremes of violence could be avoided by education, and for this reason the *Republic* is silent on the subject both of how the philosopher is to attain power and of the details of political organization. We can, however,[9] fill in the gaps in the *Republic* from the history of Plato's and Dion's experiences in Sicily. Plato lived in aristocratic circles and his pupils were chiefly drawn from the sons of tyrants or leading aristocratic politicians. It seemed possible, therefore, that the "dictatorship of the best" could be achieved without violent revolution if these young men could gain control in their respective cities. The Academy would then become the central advisory bureau for a network of aristocratic dictatorships, settling the general lines of policy on which each of the scholar-statesmen should proceed. It would be the headquarters of an "open conspiracy" to clean up Greek politics, the *Republic* would be its manifesto, and Plato the commander-in-chief.

This plan was no Utopian dream. Dion was a force in Sicilian affairs, Archytas in South Italy, and from many other cities came requests for Plato's advice and guidance. It seemed possible that the new university might really convert the rulers in nondemocratic cities and make the kings philosophers. Plato disregarded the problem of how to capture power not because he was an unpractical dreamer, but because, in the revolution of which he dreamed, the capture of power would not prove difficult. He did not wish to turn out a ruling class, but to convert it. For this reason he paid little attention to the democracies, even to Athens. There he knew his chances were

[9] See Chapter 10 [of Crossman's book].

small. Only where an oligarchy or a military dictator was in control had he a real possibility of achieving his goal, since here political power was in the hands of a few men of his own social class.

The real problems, therefore, were firstly the conversion of the Greek gentleman to Platonic philosophy, and secondly the pacification of a proletariat avid for self-government. These are the practical questions which the *Republic* tries to answer, and both are in a sense educational. Of the first we have already spoken. . . . But the second is no less important. The civilian must be educated to accept his subjection to the rule of law. But since he is naturally incapable of philosophy or of directing his life according to reason and cannot understand the *raison d'être* of the State, it is useless to explain the truth to him. He must therefore be fed on political and religious myths, "noble lies" as Plato called them, which appeal to his emotions and stimulate him to obey the law.

By the "noble lie" Plato meant propaganda, the technique of controlling the behavior of the stupid majority: and he believed that this was the only sort of general education which the civilian should receive. He must, in fact, be content with the education which Plato had prepared for the children of the ruling class, since politically and morally he would always remain a child. Just as children are told improving stories to prevent them from biting their nails or stealing or telling lies, so the civilian must be fed on propaganda to prevent him from asserting his right to self-government. One such story Plato himself suggested:

> "Yes," I said, "you are no doubt right; but still listen to the rest of the tale. 'You in this city are all brothers'—thus we shall tell our tale to them—'but God, as he was fashioning you, put gold in those of you who are capable of ruling; hence they are deserving of most reverence. He put silver in the auxiliaries, and iron and copper in the farmers and the other craftsmen. For the most part your children are of the same nature as yourselves, but because you are all akin, sometimes from gold will come a silver offspring, or from silver a gold, and so on all round. Therefore the first and weightiest command of God to the rulers is this—that more than aught else they be good guardians of and watch zealously over the offspring, seeing which of those metals is mixed in their souls; if their own offspring have an admixture

of copper or iron, they must show no pity, but giving it the honor proper to its nature, set it among the artisans or the farmers; and if on the other hand in these classes children are born with an admixture of gold and silver, they shall do them honor and appoint the first to be guardians, the second to be auxiliaries. For there is an oracle that the city shall perish when it is guarded by iron or copper.' " [10]

Philosophy for the ruler, and propaganda for the rest—this, says Plato, is the best way of avoiding bloodshed in the establishment and maintenance of the "dictatorship of the best." The mistake of Socrates had been his belief that the Law of Reason was suitable for everyone. He had condemned rhetoric and sophistical education altogether and tried to convert the city of Athens to philosophy. But philosophy and reason are poison to the masses. Misunderstood and perverted by them, they merely intensify social unrest. The masses need not the truth, but a convenient falsehood. They, like Adam and Eve, must be forbidden to eat of the Tree of the Knowledge of Good and Evil—for their own sakes. The philosopher-king therefore will not condemn propaganda altogether, but will demand the absolute control of it by the Government. Literature, music, religion, science —everything which can disturb their minds must be censored by the rulers and regulated so as to promote the loyalty of the masses to the new regime. The perfect State will be for the civilian quite literally 'a fool's paradise,' controlled by a few wise men, who out of their compassion for the masses provide them with superstitions and ceremonies and popular philosophies fit for their feeble capacities.[11]

Plato's philosophy is the most savage and the most profound attack upon liberal ideas which history can show. It denies every axiom of "progressive" thought and challenges all its fondest ideals. Equality, freedom, self-government—all are condemned as illusions which can be held only by idealists whose sympathies are stronger than their sense. The true idealist, on Plato's view, will see men as they are, observe their radical inequalities, and give to the many not self-government but security, not freedom but prosperity, not knowledge but

---

[10] *Republic*, 415, Lindsay's translation. For a macabre modern parallel compare Hitler's speech at the Nuremberg Rally in 1934.

[11] Cf. "The Grand Inquisitor" in *The Brothers Karamazov*, where the same theory is worked out.

the "noble lie." The perfect State is not a democracy of rational equals, but an aristocracy in which a hereditary caste of cultured gentlemen care with paternal solicitude for the toiling masses.

Before the First World War, the *Republic* was often treated as the "Ideal State" which Plato never intended to put into practice. Its whole conception seemed far-fetched and remote to a generation which assumed liberal ideas as self-evident truths of human nature. A world which believed that, under the flags of science, general education, and democracy, it was marching to perfection, could not swallow Plato's estimate of the common man, or seriously approve his educational program. Unaware of the class war, it could not understand his hatred of democracy and acceptance of dictatorship. But because Plato was a famous philosopher, he was rarely condemned outright as a reactionary resolutely opposed to every principle of the liberal creed. Instead, he was elevated to a higher rank, and became an idealist, remote from practical life, dreaming of a transcendent City of God.

World war has changed all that. Plato's so-called "idealism" is now seen for what it is—a grimly realistic estimate of the moral and intellectual capacities of the masses. Knowing what class war and revolution mean, we can understand why Plato advocated dictatorship to prevent them. Having some experience of the effects of propaganda, we can treat "the noble lie" not as an amusing fantasy but as an extremely practical instrument of government. Our modern objection to Plato is that he is much too "realistic" in his analysis of human nature.

PLATO AS ENEMY OF THE OPEN SOCIETY
Karl R. Popper

Totalitarian justice

The analysis of Plato's sociology makes it easy to present his political program. His fundamental demands can be expressed in either of two formulas, the first corresponding to his idealist theory of change and rest, the second to his naturalism. The idealist formula is: *Arrest all political change!* Change is evil, rest divine. All change can be arrested if the state is made an exact copy of its original, i.e., of the Form or Idea of the city. Should it be asked how this is practicable, we can reply with the naturalistic formula: *Back to nature!* Back to the original state of our forefathers, the primitive state founded in accordance with human nature, and therefore stable; back to the tribal patriarchy of the time before the Fall, to the natural class rule of the wise few over the ignorant many.

I believe that nearly all the elements of Plato's political program can be derived from these demands. They are, in turn, based upon his historicism; and they have to be combined with his sociological doctrines concerning the conditions for the stability of class rule. The principal elements I have in mind are:

Karl R. Popper *is Professor of Logic and Scientific Method at the University of London. "Plato as Enemy of the Open Society" consists of the major portion of chapters 6, 7, and 8 of his* The Open Society and Its Enemies (*Princeton, N.J.: Princeton University Press, 1950*). *Copyright* © *1950 by Princeton University Press. Reprinted by permission of Princeton University Press. Popper's extensive footnotes are here omitted.*

41

(*a*) The strict division of the classes; i.e., the ruling class consisting of herdsmen and watch-dogs must be strictly separated from the human cattle.

(*b*) The identification of the fate of the state with that of the ruling class; the exclusive interest in this class, and in its unity; and subservient to this unity, the rigid rules for breeding and educating this class, and the strict supervision and collectivization of the interests of its members.

From these principal elements, others can be derived, for instance the following:

(*c*) The ruling class has a monopoly of things like military virtues and training, and of the right to carry arms and to receive education of any kind; but it is excluded from any participation in economic activities, and especially from earning money.

(*d*) There must be a censorship of all intellectual activities of the ruling class, and a continual propaganda aiming at molding and unifying their minds. All innovation in education, legislation, and religion must be prevented or suppressed.

(*e*) The state must be self-sufficient. It must aim at economic autarky; for otherwise the rulers would either be dependent upon traders, or become traders themselves. The first of these alternatives would undermine their power, the second their unity and the stability of the state.

This program can, I think, be fairly described as totalitarian. And it is certainly founded upon a historicist sociology.

But is that all? Are there no other features of Plato's program, elements which are neither totalitarian nor founded upon historicism? What about Plato's ardent desire for Goodness and Beauty, or his love of Wisdom and of Truth? What about his demand that the wise, the philosophers, should rule? What about his hopes of making the citizens of his state virtuous as well as happy? And what about his demand that the state should be founded upon Justice? Even writers who criticize Plato believe that his political doctrine, in spite of certain similarities, is clearly distinguished from modern totalitarianism by these aims of his, the happiness of the citizens, and the rule of justice. Crossman, for instance, whose critical attitude can be gauged from his remark that "Plato's philosophy is the most savage and most profound attack upon liberal ideas which history can show," seems still to believe that Plato's plan is "the building of a perfect state in which every citizen is really happy." Another example is Joad who discusses the similarities between Plato's program and that of fascism at some length, but who asserts that there are fundamental differences, since in Plato's best state "the ordinary man . . . achieves such happiness as appertains to his nature," and since this state is built upon the ideas of "an absolute good and an absolute justice."

In spite of such arguments I believe that Plato's political program, far from being morally superior to totalitarianism, is fundamentally identical with it. I believe that the objections against this view are based upon an ancient and deep-rooted prejudice in favor of idealizing Plato. That Crossman has done much to point out and to destroy this inclination may be seen from this statement: "Before the Great War . . . Plato . . . was rarely condemned outright as a reactionary, resolutely opposed to every principle of the liberal creed. Instead he was elevated to a higher rank, . . . removed from practical life, dreaming of a transcendent City of God." Crossman himself, however, is not free from that tendency which he so clearly exposes. It is interesting that this tendency could persist for such a long time in spite of the fact that Grote and Gomperz had pointed out the reactionary character of some doctrines of the *Republic* and the *Laws*. But even they did not see all the implications of these doctrines; they never doubted that Plato was, fundamentally, a humanitarian. And their adverse criticism was ignored, or interpreted as a failure to understand and to appreciate Plato who was by Christians considered a "Christian before Christ," and by revolutionaries a revolutionary. This kind of complete faith in Plato is undoubtedly still dominant, and Field, for instance, finds it necessary to warn his readers that "we shall misunderstand Plato entirely if we think of him as a revolutionary thinker." This is, of course, very true; and it would clearly be pointless if the tendency to make of Plato a revolutionary thinker, or at least a progressivist, were not fairly widespread. But Field himself has the same kind of faith in Plato; for when he goes on to say that Plato was "in strong opposition to the new and subversive tendencies" of his time, then surely he accepts too readily Plato's testimony for the subversiveness of these new tendencies. The enemies of freedom have always charged its defenders with subversion. And nearly always they have succeeded in persuading the guileless and well-meaning.

The idealization of the great idealist permeates not only the interpretations of Plato's writings, but also the translations. Drastic remarks of Plato's which do not fit the translator's views of what a humanitarian should say are frequently either toned down or misunderstood. This tendency begins with the translation of the very title of Plato's so-called "Republic." What comes first to our mind when hearing this title is that the author must be a liberal, if not a revolutionary. But the title "Republic" is, quite simply, the English form of the Latin rendering of a Greek word that had no associations of this kind, and whose proper English translation would be "The Constitution" or "The City-State" or "The State." The traditional translation "The Republic" has undoubtedly contributed to the general conviction that Plato could not have been a reactionary.

In view of all that Plato says about Goodness and Justice and the other Ideas mentioned, my thesis that his political demands are purely totalitarian and antihumanitarian needs to be defended. In order to undertake this defense, I shall . . . concentrate upon a critical examination of the ethical Ideas mentioned, and of their part in Plato's political demands. . . .

I

What do we really mean when we speak of "Justice"? I do not think that verbal questions of this kind are particularly important, or that it is possible to make a definite answer to them, since such terms are always used in various senses. However, I think that most of us, especially those whose general outlook is humanitarian, mean something like this: (a) an equal distribution of the burden of citizenship, i.e., of those limitations of freedom which are necessary in social life; (b) equal treatment of the citizens before the law, provided, of course, that (c) the laws show neither favor nor disfavor toward individual citizens or groups or classes; (d) impartiality of the courts of justice; and (e) an equal share in the advantages (and not only in the burden) which membership of the state may offer to its citizens. If Plato had meant by "justice" anything of this kind, then my claim that his program is purely totalitarian would certainly be wrong and all those would be right who believe that Plato's politics rested upon an acceptable humanitarian basis. But the fact is that he meant by "justice" something entirely different.

What did Plato mean by "justice"? I assert that in the *Republic* he used the term "just" as a synonym for "that which is in the interest of the best state." And what is in the interest of this best state? To arrest all change, by the maintenance of a rigid class division and class rule. If I am right in this interpretation, then we should have to say that Plato's demand for justice leaves his political program at the level of totalitarianism; and we should have to conclude that we must guard against the danger of being impressed by mere words.

Justice is the central topic of the *Republic*; in fact, "On Justice" is its traditional subtitle. In his enquiry into the nature of justice . . . he first tries to search for this Idea in the state, and then attempts to apply the result to the individual. One cannot say that Plato's question "What is justice?" quickly finds an answer, for it is given only in the Fourth Book. The considerations which lead up to it will be analyzed more fully later in this chapter. Briefly, they are as follows:

The city is founded upon human nature, its needs, and its limitations. "We have stated, and, you will remember, repeated over and over again that each man in our city should do one work only; namely, that work for which his nature is naturally best fitted." From this Plato concludes that everyone should mind his own business; that the carpenter should confine himself to carpentering, the shoemaker to making shoes. Not much harm is done, however, if two workers change their natural places. "But should anyone who is by nature a worker (or else a member of the money-earning class) . . . manage to get into the warrior class; or should a warrior get into the class of the guardians, without being worthy of it; . . . then this kind of change and of underhand plotting would mean the downfall of the city." From this argument which is closely related to the principle that the carrying of arms should be a class prerogative, Plato draws his final conclusion that any changing or intermingling within the three classes must be injustice, and that the opposite therefore, is justice: "When each class in the city minds its own business, the money-earning class

as well as the auxiliaries and the guardians, then this will be justice."
This conclusion is reaffirmed and summed up a little later: "The city
is just . . . if each of its three classes attends to its own work." But
this statement means that Plato identifies justice with the principle
of class rule and of class privilege. For the principle that every class
should attend to its own business means, briefly and bluntly, that
*the state is just if the ruler rules, if the worker works, and if the slave
slaves.*

It will be seen that Plato's concept of justice is fundamentally different from our ordinary view as analyzed above. Plato calls class
privilege "just," while we usually mean by justice rather the absence
of such privilege. But the difference goes further than that. We mean
by justice some kind of equality in the treatment of *individuals,*
while Plato considers justice not as a relationship between individuals,
but as a property of the *whole state,* based upon a relationship between its classes. The state is just if it is healthy, strong, united—
stable.

II

But was Plato perhaps right? Does "justice" perhaps mean
what he says? I do not intend to discuss such a question. If anyone
should hold that "justice" means the unchallenged rule of one class,
then I should simply reply that I am all for injustice. In other words,
I believe that nothing depends upon words, and everything upon our
practical demands or upon the proposals for framing our policy which
we decide to adopt. Behind Plato's definition of justice stands, fundamentally, his demand for a totalitarian class rule, and his decision to
bring it about.

But was he not right in a different sense? Did his idea of justice
perhaps correspond to the Greek way of using this word? Did the
Greeks perhaps mean by "justice," something holistic, like the "health
of the state," and is it not utterly unfair and unhistorical to expect
from Plato an anticipation of our modern idea of justice as equality
of the citizens before the law? This question, indeed, has been answered in the affirmative, and the claim has been made that Plato's
holistic idea of "social justice" is characteristic of the traditional

Greek outlook, of the "Greek genius" which "was not, like the Roman, specifically legal," but rather "specifically metaphysical." But
this claim is untenable. As a matter of fact, the Greek way of using
the word "justice" was indeed surprisingly similar to our own individualistic and equalitarian usage.

In order to show this, I may first refer to Plato himself who, in
the dialogue *Gorgias* (which is earlier than the *Republic*), speaks of
the view that "justice is equality" as one held by the great mass of
the people, and as one which agrees not only with "convention,"
but with "nature itself." I may further quote Aristotle, another opponent of equalitarianism, who, under the influence of Plato's
naturalism, elaborated among other things the theory that some
men are by nature born to slave. Nobody could be less interested in
spreading an equalitarian and individualistic interpretation of the
term "justice." But when speaking of the judge, whom he describes
as "a personification of that which is just," Aristotle says that it is
the task of the judge to "restore equality." He tells us that "all men
think justice to be a kind of equality," an equality, namely, which
"pertains to persons." He even thinks (but here he is wrong) that
the Greek word for "justice" is to be derived from a root that means
"equal division." (The view that "justice" means a kind of "equality
in the division of spoils and honors to the citizens" agrees with Plato's
views in the *Laws*, where two kinds of equality in the distribution of
spoils and honors are distinguished—"numerical" or "arithmetical"
equality and "proportionate" equality; the second of which takes account of the degree in which the persons in question possess virtue,
breeding, and wealth—and where this proportionate equality is said
to constitute "political justice.") And when Aristotle discusses the
principles of democracy, he says that "democratic justice is the application of the principle of arithmetical equality (as distinct from
proportionate equality)." All this is certainly not merely his personal
impression of the meaning of justice, nor is it perhaps only a description of the way in which the word was used, after Plato, under the
influence of the *Gorgias* and the *Laws*; it is, rather, the expression of
a universal and ancient as well as popular use of the word "justice."

In view of this evidence, we must say, I think, that the holistic
and anti-equalitarian interpretation of justice in the *Republic* was

an innovation, and that Plato attempted to present his totalitarian class rule as "just" while people generally meant by "justice" the exact opposite.

This result is startling, and opens up a number of questions. Why did Plato claim, in the *Republic*, that justice meant inequality if, in general usage, it meant equality? To me the only likely reply seems to be that he wanted to make propaganda for his totalitarian state by persuading the people that it was the "just" state. But was such an attempt worth his while, considering that it is not words but what we mean by them that matters? Of course it was worth while; this can be seen from the fact that he fully succeeded in persuading his readers, down to our own day, that he was candidly advocating justice, i.e., that justice they were striving for. And it is a fact that he thereby spread doubt and confusion among equalitarians and individualists who, under the influence of his authority, began to ask themselves whether his idea of justice was not truer and better than theirs. Since the word "justice" symbolizes to us an aim of such importance, and since so many are prepared to endure anything for it, and to do all in their power for its realization, the enlistment of these humanitarian forces, or at least, the paralyzing of equalitarianism, was certainly an aim worthy of being pursued by a believer in totalitarianism. But was Plato aware that justice meant so much to men? He was; for he writes in the *Republic*: "When a man has committed an injustice, . . . is it not true that his courage refuses to be stirred? . . . But when he believes that he has suffered injustice, does not his vigor and his wrath flare up at once? And is it not equally true that when fighting on the side of what he believes to be just, he can endure hunger and cold, and any kind of hardship? And does he not hold on until he conquers, persisting in his exalted state until he has either achieved his aim, or perished?"

Reading this, we cannot doubt that Plato knew the power of faith, and, above all, of a faith in justice. Nor can we doubt that the *Republic* must tend to pervert this faith, and to replace it by a directly opposite faith. And in the light of the available evidence, it seems to me most probable that Plato knew very well what he was doing. Equalitarianism was his arch-enemy, and he was out to destroy it; no doubt in the sincere belief that it was a great evil and a great danger.

But his attack upon equalitarianism was not an honest attack. Plato did not dare to face the enemy openly.

I proceed to present the evidence in support of this contention.

III

The *Republic* is probably the most elaborate monograph on justice ever written. It examines a variety of views about justice, and it does this in a way which leads us to believe that Plato omitted none of the more important theories known to him. In fact, Plato clearly implies that because of his vain attempts to track it down among the current views, a new search for justice is necessary. Yet in his survey and discussion of the current theories, the view that justice is equality before the law (*"isonomy"*) is never mentioned. This omission can be explained only in two ways. Either he overlooked the equalitarian theory, or he purposely avoided it. The first possibility seems very unlikely if we consider the care with which the *Republic* is composed, and the necessity for Plato to analyze the theories of his opponents if he was to make a forceful presentation of his own. But this possibility appears even more improbable if we consider the wide popularity of the equalitarian theory. We need not, however, rely upon merely probable arguments since it can be easily shown that Plato was not only acquainted with the equalitarian theory but well aware of its importance when he wrote the *Republic*. As already mentioned in this chapter (in section II), . . . equalitarianism played a considerable role in the earlier *Gorgias* where it is even defended; and in spite of the fact that the merits or demerits of equalitarianism are nowhere seriously discussed in the *Republic*, Plato did not change his mind regarding its influence, for the *Republic* itself testifies to its popularity. It is there alluded to as a very popular democratic belief; but it is treated only with scorn, and all we hear about it consists of a few sneers and pin-pricks, well matched with the abusive attack upon Athenian democracy, and made at a place where justice is not the topic of the discussion. The possibility that the equalitarian theory of justice was overlooked by Plato is therefore ruled out, and so is the possibility that he did not see that a discussion of an influential theory diametrically opposed to his own was requisite. The fact that his silence in the *Republic* is broken only by a few jocular remarks (apparently he thought them too good to be suppressed) can be explained only as a conscious refusal to discuss it. In view of all that, I do not see how Plato's method of impressing upon his readers the belief that all important theories have been examined can be reconciled with the standards of intellectual honesty; though we must add that his failure is undoubtedly due to his complete devotion to a cause in whose goodness he firmly believed.

In order to appreciate fully the implications of Plato's practically unbroken silence on this issue, we must first see clearly that the equalitarian movement as Plato knew it represented all he hated, and that his own theory, in the *Republic* and in all later works, was largely a reply to the powerful challenge of the new equalitarianism and humanitarianism. To show this, I shall discuss the main principles of the humanitarian movement, and contrast them with the corresponding principles of Platonic totalitarianism.

The humanitarian theory of justice makes three main demands or proposals, namely (*a*) the equalitarian principle proper, i.e., the proposal to eliminate "natural" privileges, (*b*) the general principle of individualism, and (*c*) the principle that it should be the task and the purpose of the state to protect the freedom of its citizens. To each of these political demands or proposals there corresponds a directly opposite principle of Platonism, namely (*a'*) the principle of natural privilege, (*b'*) the general principle of holism or collectivism, and (*c'*) the principle that it should be the task and the purpose of the individual to maintain, and to strengthen, the stability of the state.—I shall discuss these three points in order, devoting to each of them one of the sections IV, V, and VI of this chapter.

IV

Equalitarianism proper is the demand that the citizens of the state should be treated impartially. It is the demand that birth, family connection, or wealth must not influence those who administer the law to the citizens. In other words, it does not recognize any "natural" privileges, although certain privileges may be conferred by the citizens upon those they trust.

This equalitarian principle had been admirably formulated by

Pericles a few years before Plato's birth, in an oration which has been preserved by Thucydides. . . . Two of its sentences may be given here: " 'Our laws,' said Pericles, 'afford equal justice to all alike in their private disputes, but we do not ignore the claims of excellence. When a citizen distinguishes himself, then he is preferred to the public service, not as a matter of privilege, but as a reward for merit; and poverty is not a bar. . . .' " These sentences express some of the fundamental aims of the great equalitarian movement which, as we have seen, did not even shrink from attacking slavery. In Pericles' own generation, this movement was represented by Euripides, Antiphon, and Hippias, . . . and also by Herodotus. In Plato's generation, it was represented by Alcidamas and Lycophron, . . . another supporter was Antisthenes, who had been one of Socrates' closest friends.

Plato's principle of justice was, of course, diametrically opposed to all this. He demanded natural privileges for the natural leaders. But how did he contest the equalitarian principle? And how did he establish his own demands?

. . . Some of the best-known formulations of the equalitarian demands were couched in the impressive but questionable language of "natural rights," and that some of their representatives argued in favor of these demands by pointing out the "natural," i.e., biological, equality of men. We have seen that the argument is irrelevant; that men are equal in some important respects, and unequal in others; and that normative demands cannot be derived from this fact, or from any other fact. It is therefore interesting to note that the naturalist argument was not used by all equalitarians, and that Pericles, for one, did not even allude to it.

Plato quickly found that naturalism was a weak spot within the equalitarian doctrine, and he took the fullest advantage of this weakness. To tell men that they are equal has a certain sentimental appeal. But this appeal is small compared with that made by a propaganda that tells them that they are superior to others, and that others are inferior to them. Are you naturally equal to your servants, to your slaves, to the manual worker who is no better than an animal? The very question is ridiculous! Plato seems to have been the first to appreciate the possibilities of this reaction, and to oppose contempt, scorn, and ridicule to the claim to natural equality. This explains why he was anxious to impute the naturalistic argument even to those of his opponents who did not use it; in the *Menexenus*, a parody of Pericles' oration, he therefore insists on linking together the claims to equal laws and to natural equality: "The basis of our constitution is equality of birth," he says ironically. "We are all brethren, and are all children of one mother; . . . and the natural equality of birth induces us to strive for equality before the law."

Later, in the *Laws*, Plato summarizes his reply to equalitarianism in the formula: "Equal treatment of unequals must beget inequity"; and this was developed by Aristotle into the formula "Equality for equals, inequality for unequals." This formula indicates what may be termed the standard objection to equalitarianism; the objection that equality would be excellent if only men were equal, but that it is manifestly impossible since they are not equal, and since they cannot be made equal. This apparently very realistic objection is, in fact, most unrealistic, for political privileges have never been founded upon natural differences of character. And, indeed, Plato does not seem to have had much confidence in this objection when writing the *Republic*, for it is used there only in one of his sneers at democracy when he says that it "distributes equality to equals and unequals alike." Apart from this remark, he prefers not to argue against equalitarianism, but to forget it.

Summing up, it can be said that Plato never underrated the significance of the equalitarian theory, supported as it was by a man like Pericles, but that, in the *Republic*, he did not treat it at all; he attacked it, but not squarely and openly.

But how did he try to establish his own anti-equalitarianism, his principle of natural privilege? In the *Republic*, he proffered three different arguments, though two of them hardly deserve the name. The first is the surprising remark that, since all the other three virtues of the state have been examined, the remaining fourth, that of "minding one's own business," must be "justice." I am reluctant to believe that this was meant as an argument; but it must be, for Plato's leading speaker, "Socrates," introduces it by asking: "Do you know how I arrive at this conclusion?" The second argument is more interesting, for it is an attempt to show that his anti-equalitarianism can be derived from the ordinary (i.e., equalitarian) view that justice is impartiality. I quote the passage in full. Remarking that the rulers of the city will also be its judges, "Socrates" says: "And will it not be the aim of their jurisdiction that no man shall take what belongs to another, and shall be deprived of what is his own?"—"Yes," is the reply of "Glaucon," the interlocutor, "that will be their intention." —"Because that would be just?"—"Yes."—"Accordingly, to keep and to practice what belongs to us and is our own will be generally agreed upon to be justice." Thus it is established that "to keep and to practice what is one's own" is the principle of just jurisdiction, according to our ordinary ideas of justice. Here the second argument ends, giving way to the third (to be analyzed below) which leads to the conclusion that it is justice to keep one's own station (or to do one's own business), which is the station (or the business) of one's own class or caste.

The sole purpose of this second argument is to impress upon the reader that "justice," in the ordinary sense of the word, requires us to keep our own station, since we should always keep what belongs to us. That is to say, Plato wishes his readers to draw the inference: "It is just to keep and to practice what is one's own. My place (or my business) is my own. Thus it is just for me to keep to my place (or to practice my business)." This is about as sound as the argument: "It is just to keep and to practice what is one's own. This plan of stealing your money is my own. Thus it is just for me to keep to my plan, and to put it into practice, i.e., to steal your money." It is clear that the inference which Plato wishes us to draw is nothing but a crude juggle with the meaning of the term "one's own." (For the problem is whether justice demands that everything which is in some sense "our own," e.g., "our own" class, should therefore be treated, not only as our possession, but as our inalienable possession. But in such a principle Plato himself does not believe; for it would clearly make a transition to communism impossible. And what about keeping our own children?) This crude juggle is Plato's way of establishing what Adam calls "a point of contact between his own view of Justice and the popular . . . meaning of the word." This is how the greatest philosopher of all time tries to convince us that he has discovered the true nature of justice.

The third and last argument which Plato offers is much more serious. It is an appeal to the principle of holism or collectivism, and is connected with the principle that it is the end of the individual to maintain the stability of the state. It will therefore be discussed, in this analysis, below, in sections v and vi.

But before proceeding to these points, I wish to draw attention to the "preface" which Plato places before his description of the "discovery" which we are here examining. It must be considered in the light of the observations we have made so far. Viewed in this light, the "lengthy preface"—this is how Plato himself describes it—appears as an ingenious attempt to prepare the reader for the "discovery of justice" by making him believe that there is an argument going on when in reality he is only faced with a display of dramatic devices, designed to soothe his critical faculties.

Having discovered wisdom as the virtue proper to the guardians and courage as that proper to the auxiliaries, "Socrates" announces his intention of making a final effort to discover justice. "Two things are left," he says, "which we shall have to discover in the city: temperance, and finally that other thing which is the main object of all our investigations, namely justice."—"Exactly," says Glaucon. Socrates now suggests that temperance shall be dropped. But Glaucon protests and Socrates gives in, saying that "it would be dishonest if I were to refuse." This little dispute prepares the reader for the reintroduction of justice, suggests to him that Socrates possesses the means for its "discovery," and reassures him that Glaucon is carefully watching Plato's intellectual honesty in conducting the argument which he, the reader himself, need not therefore watch at all.

Socrates next proceeds to discuss temperance, which he discovers to be the only virtue proper to the workers. (By the way, the much debated question whether Plato's "justice" is distinguishable from his "temperance" can be easily answered. Justice means *to keep one's place*; temperance means *to know one's place*—that is to say, more precisely, to be satisfied with it. What other virtue could be proper to the workers who fill their bellies like the beasts?) When temperance has been discovered, Socrates asks: "And what about the last principle? Obviously it will be justice."—"Obviously," replies Glaucon.

"Now, my dear Glaucon," says Socrates, "we must, like hunters, surround her cover and keep a close watch, and we must not allow her to escape, and to get away; for surely, justice must be somewhere near this spot. You had better look out and search the place. And if you are the first to see her, then give me a shout!" Glaucon, like the

reader, is of course unable to do anything of the sort, and implores
Socrates to take the lead. "Then offer your prayers with me," says
Socrates, "and follow me." But even Socrates finds the ground "hard
to traverse, since it is covered with underwood; it is dark, and difficult to explore. . . . But," he says, "we must go on with it." And
instead of protesting "Go on with what? With our exploration, i.e.,
with our argument? But we have not even started. There has not been
a glimmer of sense in what you have said so far," Glaucon, and the
naïve reader with him, replies meekly: "Yes, we must go on." Now
Socrates reports that he has "got a glimpse" (we have not), and gets
excited. "Hurray! Hurray!" he cries, "Glaucon! There seems to be a
track! I think now that the quarry will not escape us!"—"That is
good news," replies Glaucon. "Upon my word," says Socrates, "we
have made utter fools of ourselves. What we were looking for at a
distance, has been lying at our very feet all the time! And we never
saw it!" With exclamations and repeated assertions of this kind,
Socrates continues for a good while, interrupted by Glaucon, who
gives expression to the reader's feelings and asks Socrates what he
has found. But when Socrates says only "We have been talking of it
all the time, without realizing that we were actually describing it,"
Glaucon expresses the reader's impatience and says: "This preface
gets a bit lengthy; remember that I want to hear what it is all about."
And only then does Plato proceed to proffer the two "arguments"
which I have outlined.

Glaucon's last remark may be taken as an indication that Plato
was conscious of what he was doing in this "lengthy preface." I
cannot interpret it as anything but an attempt—it proved to be highly
successful—to lull the reader's critical faculties, and, by means of a
dramatic display of verbal fireworks, to divert his attention from the
intellectual poverty of this masterly piece of dialogue. One is tempted
to think that Plato knew its weakness, and how to hide it.

V

The problem of individualism and collectivism is closely
related to that of equality and inequality. Before going on to discuss
it, a few terminological remarks seem to be necessary.

The term "individualism" can be used (according to the *Oxford*

Dictionary) in two different ways: (*a*) in opposition to collectivism, and (*b*) in opposition to altruism. There is no other word to express the former meaning, but several synonyms for the latter, for example "egoism" or "selfishness." This is why in what follows I shall use the term "individualism" *exclusively* in sense (*a*), using terms like "egoism" or "selfishness" if sense (*b*) is intended. A little table may be useful:

(*a*) *Individualism*   is opposed to   (*a'*) *Collectivism.*
(*b*) *Egoism*   is opposed to   (*b'*) *Altruism.*

Now these four terms describe certain attitudes, or demands, or decisions, or proposals, for codes of normative laws. Though necessarily vague, they can, I believe, be easily illustrated by examples and so be used with a precision sufficient for our present purpose. Let us begin with collectivism. . . . "The part exists for the sake of the whole, but the whole does not exist for the sake of the part. . . . You are created for the sake of the whole and not the whole for the sake of you." This quotation not only illustrates holism and collectivism, but also conveys its strong emotional appeal of which Plato was conscious (as can be seen from the preamble to the passage). The appeal is to various feelings, e.g., the longing to belong to a group or a tribe; and one factor in it is the moral appeal for altruism and against selfishness. Plato suggests that if you cannot sacrifice your interests for the sake of the whole, then you are selfish.

Now a glance at our little table will show that this is not so. Collectivism is not opposed to egoism, nor is it identical with altruism or unselfishness. Collective or group egoism, for instance class egoism, is a very common thing (Plato knew this very well), and this shows clearly enough that collectivism as such is not opposed to selfishness. On the other hand, an anti-collectivist, i.e., an individualist, can, at the same time, be an altruist; he can be ready to make sacrifices in order to help other individuals. One of the best examples of this attitude is perhaps Dickens. It would be difficult to say which is the stronger, his passionate hatred of selfishness or his passionate interest in individuals with all their human weaknesses; and this attitude is combined with a dislike, not only of what we now call collective bodies or collectives, but even of a genuinely devoted altruism, if directed toward anonymous groups rather than concrete individuals. (I remind the reader of Mrs. Jellyby in *Bleak House*, "a lady devoted to public duties.") These illustrations, I think, explain sufficiently clearly the meaning of our four terms; and they show that any of the terms in our table can be combined with either of the two terms that stand in the other line (which gives four possible combinations).

Now it is interesting that for Plato, and for most Platonists, an altruistic individualism (as for instance that of Dickens) cannot exist. According to Plato, the only alternative to collectivism is egoism; he simply identifies all altruism with collectivism, and all individualism with egoism. This is not a matter of terminology, of mere words, for instead of four possibilities, Plato recognized only two. This has created considerable confusion in speculation on ethical matters, even down to our own day.

Plato's identification of individualism with egoism furnishes him with a powerful weapon for his defense of collectivism as well as for his attack upon individualism. In defending collectivism, he can appeal to our humanitarian feeling of unselfishness; in his attack, he can brand all individualists as selfish, as incapable of devotion to anything but themselves. This attack, although aimed by Plato against individualism in our sense, i.e., against the rights of human individuals, reaches of course only a very different target, egoism. But this difference is constantly ignored by Plato and by most Platonists.

Why did Plato try to attack individualism? I think he knew very well what he was doing when he trained his guns upon this position, for individualism, perhaps even more than equalitarianism, was a stronghold in the defenses of the new humanitarian creed. The emancipation of the individual was indeed the great spiritual revolution which had led to the breakdown of tribalism and to the rise of democracy. Plato's uncanny sociological intuition shows itself in the way in which he invariably discerned the enemy wherever he met him.

Individualism was part of the old intuitive idea of justice. That justice is not, as Plato would have it, the health and harmony of the state, but rather a certain way of treating individuals, is emphasized by Aristotle, it will be remembered, when he says "justice is something that pertains to persons." This individualistic element had been emphasized by the generation of Pericles. Pericles himself made it clear that the laws must guarantee equal justice "to all alike in their private disputes"; but he went further. "We do not feel called upon," he said, "to nag at our neighbor if he chooses to go his own way." (Compare this with Plato's remark that the state does not produce men "for the purpose of letting them loose, each to go his own way. . . .") Pericles insists that this individualism must be linked with altruism: "We are taught . . . never to forget that we must protect the injured"; and his speech culminates in a description of the young Athenian who grows up "to a happy versatility, and to self-reliance."

This individualism, united with altrusm, has become the basis of our western civilizaton. It is the central doctrine of Christianity ("love your neighbor," say the Scriptures, not "love your tribe"); and it is the core of all ethical doctrines which have grown from our civilization and stimulated it. It is also, for instance, Kant's central practical doctrine ("always recognize that human individuals are ends, and do not use them as mere means to your ends"). There is no other thought which has been so powerful in the moral development of man.

Plato was right when he saw in this doctrine the enemy of his caste state; and he hated it more than any other of the "subversive" doctrines of his time. In order to show this even more clearly, I shall quote two passages from the *Laws* whose truly astonishing hostility towards the individual is, I think, too little appreciated. The first of them is famous as a reference to the *Republic*, whose "community of women and children and property" it discusses. Plato describes here the constitution of the *Republic* as "the highest form of the state." In this highest state, he tells us, "there is common property of wives, of children, and of all chattels. And everything possible has been done to eradicate from our life everywhere and in every way all that is private and individual. So far as it can be done, even those things which nature herself has made private and individual have somehow become the common property of all. Our very eyes and ears and hands seem to see, to hear, and to act, as if they belonged not to individuals but to the community. All men are molded to be unanimous in the utmost degree in bestowing praise and blame, and they even rejoice and grieve about the same things, and at the same time. And all the laws are perfected for unifying the city to the utmost." Plato goes on to say that "no man can find a better criterion of the highest excellence of a state than the principles just expounded"; and he describes such a state as "divine," and as the "model" or "pattern" or "original" of the state, i.e., as its Form or Idea. This is Plato's own view of the *Republic*, expressed at a time when he had given up hope of realizing his political ideal in all its glory.

The second passage, also from the *Laws*, is, if possible, even more outspoken. It should be emphasized that the passage deals primarily with military expeditions and with military discipline, but Plato leaves no doubt that these same militarist principles should be adhered to not only in war, but also "in peace, and from the earliest childhood on." Like other totalitarian militarists and admirers of Sparta, Plato urges that the all-important requirements of military discipline must be paramount, even in peace, and that they must determine the whole life of all citizens; for not only the full citizens (who are all soldiers) and the children, but also the very beasts must spend their whole life in a state of permanent and total mobilization. "The greatest principle of all," he writes, "is that nobody, whether male or female, should ever be without a leader. Nor should the mind of anybody be habituated to letting him do anything at all on his own initiative, neither out of zeal, nor even playfully. But in war and in the midst of peace—to his leader he shall direct his eye, and follow him faithfully. And even in the smallest matters he should stand under leadership. For example, he should get up, or move, or wash, or take his meals . . . only if he has been told to do so. . . . In a word, he should teach his soul, by long habit, never to dream of acting independently, and to become utterly incapable of it. In this way the life of all will be spent in total community. There is no law, nor will there ever be one, which is superior to this, or better and more effective in ensuring salvation and victory in war. *And in times of peace, and from the earliest childhood on should* it be fostered—this habit of ruling others, and of being ruled by others. And every trace of anarchy should be utterly eradicated from the life of all the men, and even of the wild beasts which are subject to men."

These are strong words. Never was a man more in earnest in his hostility toward the individual. And this hatred is deeply rooted in the fundamental dualism of Plato's philosophy; he hated the individual and his freedom just as he hated the varying particular experiences, the variety of the changing world of sensible things. In the field of politics, the individual is to Plato the Evil One himself.

This attitude, antihumanitarian and anti-Christian as it is, has been consistently idealized. It has been interpreted as humane, as unselfish, as altruistic, and as Christian. E. B. England, for instance, calls the first of these two passages from the *Laws* "a vigorous denunciation of selfishness." Similar words are used by Barker, when discussing Plato's theory of justice. He says that Plato's aim was "to replace selfishness and civil discord by harmony," and that "the old harmony of the interests of the State and the individual . . . is thus restored in the teachings of Plato; but restored on a new and higher level, because it has been elevated into a conscious sense of harmony." Such statements and countless similar ones can be easily explained if we remember Plato's identification of individualism with egoism; for all these Platonists believe that anti-individualism is the same as selflessness. This illustrates my contention that this identification had the effect of a successful piece of antihumanitarian propaganda, and that it has confused speculation on ethical matters down to our own time. But we must also realize that those who, deceived by this identification and by high-sounding words, exalt Plato's reputation as a teacher of morals and announce to the world that his ethics is the nearest approach to Christianity before Christ, are preparing the way for totalitarianism and especially for a totalitarian, anti-Christian interpretation of Christianity. And this is a dangerous thing, for there have been times when Christianity was dominated by totalitarian ideas. There was an Inquisition; and, in another form, it may come again.

It may therefore be worth while to mention some further reasons why guileless people have persuaded themselves of the humaneness of Plato's intentions. One is that when preparing the ground for his collectivist doctrines, Plato usually begins by quoting a maxim or proverb (which seems to be of Pythagorean origin): "Friends have in common all things they possess." This is, undoubtedly, an unselfish, high-minded, and excellent sentiment. Who could suspect that an argument starting from such a commendable assumption would arrive at a wholly antihumanitarian conclusion? Another and important point is that there are many genuinely humanitarian sentiments expressed in Plato's dialogues, particularly in those written before the *Republic* when he was still under the influence of Socrates. I mention especially Socrates' doctrine, in the *Gorgias*, that it is worse to do injustice than to suffer it. Clearly, this doctrine is not only altruistic, but also individualistic; for in a collectivist theory of justice like that of the *Republic*, injustice is an act against the state, not against a particular man, and though a man may commit an act of injustice, only the collective can suffer from it. But in the *Gorgias* we find nothing of the kind. The theory of justice is a perfectly normal one, and the examples of injustice given by "Socrates" (who has here probably a good deal of the real Socrates in him) are such as boxing a man's ears, injuring, or killing him. Socrates' teaching that it is better to suffer such acts than to do them is indeed very similar to Christian teaching, and his doctrine of justice fits in excellently with the spirit of Pericles. . . .

Now the *Republic* develops a new doctrine of justice which is not only incompatible with such an individualism, but utterly hostile toward it. But a reader may easily believe that Plato is still holding fast to the doctrine of the *Gorgias*. For in the *Republic*, Plato frequently alludes to the doctrine that it is better to suffer than to commit injustice, in spite of the fact that this is simply nonsense from the point of view of the collectivist theory of justice proffered in this work. Furthermore, we hear in the *Republic* the opponents of "Socrates" giving voice to the opposite theory, that it is good and pleasant to inflict injustice, and bad to suffer it. Of course, every humanitarian is repelled by such cynicism, and when Plato formulates his aims through the mouth of Socrates: "I fear to commit a sin if I permit such evil talk about Justice in my presence, without doing my utmost to defend her," then the trusting reader is convinced of Plato's good intentions, and ready to follow him wherever he goes.

The effect of this assurance of Plato's is much enhanced by the fact that it follows, and is contrasted with, the cynical and selfish speeches of Thrasymachus, who is depicted as a political desperado of the worst kind. At the same time, the reader is led to identify individualism with the views of Thrasymachus, and to think that Plato, in his fight against it, is fighting against all the subversive and nihilistic tendencies of his time. But we should not allow ourselves to be frightened by an individualist bogy such as Thrasymachus (there is a great similarity between his portrait and the modern collectivist bogy of "bolshevism") into accepting another more real and more dangerous because less obvious form of barbarism. For Plato replaces Thrasymachus' doctrine that the individual's might is right by the equally barbaric doctrine that right is everything that furthers the stability and the might of the state.

To sum up. Because of his radical collectivism, Plato is not even interested in those problems which men usually call the problems of justice, that is to say, in the impartial weighing of the contesting claims of individuals. Nor is he interested in adjusting the individual's claims to those of the state. For the individual is altogether inferior. "I legislate with a view to what is best for the whole state," says Plato, ". . . for I justly place the interests of the individual on an inferior level of value." He is concerned solely with the collective whole as such, and justice, to him, is nothing but the health, unity, and stability of the collective body.

VI

So far, we have seen that humanitarian ethics demands an equalitarian and individualistic interpretation of justice; but we have not yet outlined the humanitarian view of the state as such. On the other hand, we have seen that Plato's theory of the state is totalitarian; but we have not yet explained the application of this theory to the ethics of the individual. Both these tasks will be undertaken now, the second first; and I shall begin by analyzing the third of Plato's arguments in his "discovery" of justice, an argument which has so far been sketched only very roughly. Here is Plato's third argument:

"Now see whether you agree with me," says Socrates. "Do you think it would do much harm to the city if a carpenter started making shoes and a shoemaker carpentering?"—"Not very much."—"But should one who is by nature a worker, or a member of the money-earning class . . . manage to get into the warrior class; or should a warrior get into the guardians' class without being worthy of it; then this kind of change and of underhand plotting would mean the downfall of the city?"—"Most definitely it would."—"We have three classes in our city, and I take it that any such plotting or changing from one class to another is a great crime against the city, and may rightly be denounced as the utmost wickedness?"—"Assuredly."— "But you will certainly declare that utmost wickedness toward one's own city is injustice?"—"Certainly."—"Then this is injustice. And conversely, we shall say that when each class in the city attends to its own business, the money-earning class as well as the auxiliaries and the guardians, then this will be justice."

Now if we look at this argument, we find (a) the sociological assumption that any relaxing of the rigid caste system must lead to the downfall of the city; (b) the constant reiteration of the one argument that what harms the city is injustice; and (c) the inference that the opposite is justice. Now we may grant here the sociological assumption (a) since it is Plato's ideal to arrest social change, and since he means by "harm" anything that may lead to change; and it is probably quite true that social change can be arrested only by a caste system. And we may further grant the inference (c) that the opposite of injustice is justice. Of greater interest, however, is (b); a glance at Plato's argument will show that his whole trend of thought is dominated by the question: does this thing harm the city? Does it do much harm or little harm? He constantly reiterates that what threatens to harm the city is morally wicked and unjust.

We see here that Plato recognizes only one ultimate standard, the interest of the state. Everything that furthers it is good and virtuous and just; everything that threatens it is bad and wicked and unjust. Actions that serve it are moral; actions that endanger it, immoral. In other words, Plato's moral code is strictly utilitarian; it is a code of collectivist or political utilitarianism. *The criterion of morality is the interest of the state.* Morality is nothing but political hygiene.

This is the collectivist, the tribal, the totalitarian theory of morality: "Good is what is in the interest of my group; or my tribe; or my state." It is easy to see what this morality implied for international relations: that the state itself can never be wrong in any of its actions, as long as it is strong; that the state has the right, not only to do violence to its citizens, should that lead to an increase of strength, but also to attack other states, provided it does so without weakening itself. (This inference, the explicit recognition of the amorality of the state, and consequently the defense of moral nihilism in international relations, was drawn by Hegel.)

From the point of view of totalitarian ethics, from the point of view of collective utility, Plato's theory of justice is perfectly correct. To keep one's place *is* a virtue. It is that civil virtue which corresponds exactly to the military virtue of discipline. And this virtue plays exactly that role which "justice" plays in Plato's system of virtues. For the cogs in the great clockwork of the state can show "virtue" in two ways. First, they must be fit for their task, by virtue of their size, shape, strength, and so forth; and secondly, they must be fitted each into its right place and must retain that place. The first type of virtues, fitness for a specific task, will lead to a differentiation, in accordance with the specific task of the cog. Certain cogs will be virtuous, i.e., fit, only if they are ("by their nature") large; others if they are strong; and others if they are smooth. But the virtue of keeping to one's place will be common to all of them; and it will at the same time be a virtue of the whole: that of being properly fitted together—of being in harmony. To this universal virtue Plato gives the name "justice." This procedure is perfectly consistent and it is fully justified from the point of view of totalitarian morality. If the individual is nothing but a cog, then ethics is nothing but the study of how to fit him into the whole.

I wish to make it clear that I believe in the sincerity of Plato's totalitarianism. His demand for the unchallenged domination of one class over the rest was uncompromising, but his ideal was not the maximum exploitation of the working classes by the upper class; it was the stability of the whole. The reason, however, which he gives for the need to keep the exploitation within limits, is again purely utilitarian. It is the interest of stabilizing the class rule. Should the guardians try to get too much, he argues, then they will in the end have nothing at all. "If they are not satisfied with a life of stability and security, . . . and are tempted, by their power, to appropriate for themselves all the wealth of the city, then surely they are bound to find out how wise Hesiod was when he said, 'the half is more than the whole.'" But we must realize that even this tendency to restrict the exploitation of class privileges is a fairly common ingredient of totalitarianism. Totalitarianism is not simply amoral. It is the morality of the closed society—of the group, or of the tribe; it is not individual selfishness, but it is collective selfishness.

Considering that Plato's third argument is straightforward and consistent, the question may be asked why he needed the "lengthy preface" as well as the two preceding arguments? Why all this uneasiness? (Platonists will of course reply that this uneasiness exists only in my imagination. That may be so. But the irrational character of the passages can hardly be explained away.) The answer to this question is, I believe, that Plato's collective clockwork would hardly have appealed to his readers if it had been presented to them in all its barrenness and meaninglessness. Plato was uneasy because he knew and feared the strength and the moral appeal of the forces he tried to break. He did not dare to challenge them, but tried to win them over for his own purposes. Whether we witness in Plato's writings a cynical and conscious attempt to employ the moral sentiments of the new humanitarianism for his own purposes, or whether we witness rather a tragic attempt to persuade his own better conscience of the evils of individualism, we shall never know. My personal impression is that the latter is the case, and that this inner conflict is the main secret of Plato's fascination. I think that Plato was moved to the depths of his soul by the new ideas, and especially by the great individualist Socrates and his martyrdom. And I think that he fought against this influence upon himself as well as upon others with all the might of his unequalled intelligence, though not always openly. This explains also why from time to time, amid all his totalitarianism, we find some humanitarian ideas. And it explains why it was possible for philosophers to represent Plato as a humanitarian.

The principle of leadership

Certain objections to our interpretation of Plato's political program have forced us into an investigation of the part played, within this program, by such moral ideas as Justice, Goodness, Beauty, Wisdom, Truth, and Happiness. . . .

We have seen that Plato's idea of justice demands, fundamentally, that the natural rulers should rule and the natural slaves should slave. It is part of the historicist demand that the state, in order to arrest all change, should be a copy of its Idea, or of its true "nature." This theory of justice indicates very clearly that Plato saw the fundamental problem of politics in the question: *Who shall rule the state?*

I

It is my conviction that by expressing the problem of politics in the form "Who should rule?" or "Whose will should be supreme?," and so on, Plato created a lasting confusion in political philosophy. It is indeed analogous to the confusion he created in the field of moral philosophy by his identification, discussed in the last chapter, of collectivism and altruism. It is clear that once the question "Who should rule?" is asked, it is hard to avoid some such reply as "the best" or "the wisest" or "the born ruler" or "he who masters the art of ruling" (or, perhaps, "The General Will" or "The Master Race" or "The Industrial Workers" or "The People"). But such a reply, convincing as it may sound—for who would advocate the rule of "the worst" or "the greatest fool" or "the born slave"?—is, as I shall try to show, quite useless.

First of all, such a reply is liable to persuade us that some fundamental problem of political theory has been solved. But if we approach political theory from a different angle, then we find that far from solving any fundamental problems, we have merely skipped over them, by assuming that the question "Who should rule?" is fundamental. For even those who share this assumption of Plato's admit that political rulers are not always sufficiently "good" or "wise" (we need not worry about the precise meaning of these terms), and that it is not at all easy to get a government on whose goodness and wisdom one can implicitly rely. If that is granted, then we must ask whether political thought should not face from the beginning the possibility of bad government; whether we should not prepare for the worst leaders, and hope for the best. But this leads to a new approach to the problem of politics, for it forces us to replace the question: *Who should rule?* by the new question: *How can we so organize political institutions that bad or incompetent rulers can be prevented from doing too much damage?*

Those who believe that the older question is fundamental, tacitly assume that political power is "essentially" unchecked. They assume that someone has the power—either an individual or a collective body, such as a class. And they assume that he who has the power can, very nearly, do what he wills, and especially that he can strengthen his power, and thereby approximate it further to an unlimited or unchecked power. They assume that political power is, essentially, sovereign. If this assumption is made, then, indeed, the question "Who is to be the sovereign?" is the only important question left.

I shall call this assumption the *theory of (unchecked) sovereignty,* using this expression not for any particular one of the various theories of sovereignty, proffered more especially by such writers as Bodin, Rousseau, or Hegel, but for the more general assumption that political power is almost unchecked, or for the demand that it ought to be so; together with the implication that the main question left is to get this power into the best hands. This theory of sovereignty is tacitly assumed in Plato's approach, and has played its role ever since. It is also implicitly assumed, for instance, by those modern writers who believe that the main problem is: Who should dictate? The capitalists or the workers?

Without entering into a detailed criticism, I wish to point out that there are serious objections against a rash and implicit acceptance of this theory. Whatever its speculative merits may appear to be, it is certainly a very unrealistic assumption. No political power has ever been unchecked, and as long as men remain human (as long as the "Brave New World" has not materialized), there can be no absolute and unrestrained political power. So long as one man cannot accumulate enough physical power in his hands to dominate all others, just so long must he depend upon his helpers. Even the most powerful tyrant depends upon his secret police, his henchmen, and his hangmen. This dependence means that his power, great as it may be, is not unchecked, and that he has to make concessions, playing one group off against another. It means that there are other political forces, other powers besides his own, and that he can exert his rule only by utilizing and pacifying them. This shows that even the extreme cases of sovereignty are never cases of pure sovereignty. They are never cases in which the will or the interest of one man (or, if there were such a thing, the will or the interest of one group) can achieve his aim directly, without giving up some of it in order to enlist powers which he cannot conquer. And in an overwhelming number of cases, the limitations of political power go much further than this.

I have stressed these empirical points, not because I wish to use them as an argument, but merely in order to avoid objections. My claim is that every theory of sovereignty omits to face a more fundamental question—the question, namely, whether we should not strive toward institutional control of the rulers by balancing their powers against other powers. This *theory of checks and balances* can at least claim careful consideration. The only objections to this claim, as far as I can see, are (*a*) that such a control is *practically* impossible, or (*b*) that it is *essentially* inconceivable since political power is essentially sovereign. Both of these dogmatic objections are, I believe, refuted by the facts; and with them fall a number of other influential views (for instance, the theory that the only alternative to the dictatorship of one class is that of another class).

In order to raise the question of institutional control of the rulers, we need not assume more than that governments are not always good or wise. But since I have said something about historical facts, I think I should confess that I feel inclined to go a little beyond this assumption. I am inclined to think that rulers have rarely been above the average, either morally or intellectually, and often below it. And I think that it is reasonable to adopt, in politics, the principle of preparing for the worst, as well as we can, though we should, of course, at the same time try to obtain the best. It appears to me madness to base all our political efforts upon the faint hope that we shall be successful in obtaining excellent, or even competent, rulers. Strongly as I feel in these matters, I must insist, however, that my criticism of the theory of sovereignty does not depend on these more personal opinions.

Apart from these personal opinions, and apart from the empirical arguments mentioned above against the general theory of sovereignty, there is also a kind of logical argument which can be used to show the inconsistency of any of the particular forms of the theory of sovereignty; more precisely, the logical argument can be given different but analogous forms to combat the theory that the wisest should rule, or else the theories that the best, or the law, or the majority, and the like, should rule. One particular form of this logical argument is directed against a too naïve version of liberalism, of democracy, and of the principle that the majority should rule; and it is somewhat similar to the well-known *"paradox of freedom"* which has been used first, and with success, by Plato. In his criticism of democracy, and in his story of the rise of the tyrant, Plato raises implicitly the following question: What if it is the will of the people that they should not rule, but a tyrant instead? The free man, Plato suggests, may exercise his absolute freedom, first by defying the laws and ultimately by defying freedom itself and by clamoring for a tyrant. This is not just

a far-fetched possibility; it has happened a number of times; and
every time it has happened, it has put in a hopeless intellectual position all those democrats who adopt, as the ultimate basis of their
political creed, the principle of the majority rule or a similar form
of the principle of sovereignty. On the one hand, the principle they
have adopted demands from them that they should oppose any but
the majority rule, and therefore the new tyranny; on the other hand,
the same principle demands from them that they should accept any
decision reached by the majority, and thus the rule of the new tyrant.
The inconsistency of their theory must, of course, paralyze their
actions. Those of us democrats who demand the institutional control
of the rulers by the ruled, and especially the right of dismissing the
government by a majority vote, must therefore base these demands
upon better grounds than a self-contradictory theory of sovereignty.
(That this is possible will be briefly shown in the next section of this
chapter.)

Plato, we have seen, came near to discovering the paradoxes of
freedom and of democracy. But what Plato and his followers overlooked is that all the other forms of the theory of sovereignty give
rise to analogous inconsistencies. *All theories of sovereignty are paradoxical.* For instance, we may have selected "the wisest" or "the best"
as a ruler. But "the wisest" in his wisdom may find that not he but
"the best" should rule, and "the best" in his goodness may perhaps
decide that "the majority" should rule. It is important to notice that
even that form of the theory of sovereignty which demands the
"Kingship of the Law" is open to the same objection. This, in fact,
has been seen very early, as Heraclitus' remark shows: "The law can
demand, too, that the will of One Man must be obeyed."

In summing up this brief criticism, one can, I believe, assert that
the theory of sovereignty is in a weak position, both empirically and
logically. The least that can be demanded is that it must not be
adopted without careful consideration of other possibilities.

II

And indeed, it is not difficult to show that a theory of democratic control can be developed which is free of the paradox of sovereignty. The theory I have in mind is one which does not proceed,

as it were, from a doctrine of the intrinsic goodness or righteousness of a majority rule, but rather from the baseness of tyranny; or more precisely, it rests upon the decision, or upon the adoption of the proposal, to avoid and to resist tyranny.

For we may distinguish two main types of government. The first type consists of governments which we can get rid of without bloodshed—for example, by way of general elections; that is to say, the social institutions provide means by which the rulers may be dismissed by the ruled, and the social traditions ensure that these institutions will not easily be destroyed by those who are in power. The second type consists of governments which the ruled cannot get rid of except by way of a successful revolution—that is to say, in most cases, not at all. I suggest the term "democracy" as a short-hand label for a government of the first type, and the term "tyranny" or "dictatorship" for the second. This, I believe, corresponds closely to traditional usage. But I wish to make clear that no part of my argument depends on the choice of these labels; and should anybody reverse this usage (as is frequently done nowadays), then I should simply say that I am in favor of what he calls "tyranny," and object to what he calls "democracy"; and I should reject as irrelevant any attempt to discover what "democracy" "really" or "essentially" means, for example, by translating the term into "the rule of the people." (For although "the people" may influence the actions of their rulers by the threat of dismissal, they never rule themselves in any concrete, practical sense.)

If we make use of the two labels as suggested, then we can now describe, as the principle of a democratic policy, the proposal to create, develop, and protect political institutions for the avoidance of tyranny. This principle does not imply that we can ever develop institutions of this kind which are faultless or foolproof, or which ensure that the policies adopted by a democratic government will be right or good or wise—or even necessarily better or wiser than the policies adopted by a benevolent tyrant. (Since no such assertions are made, the paradox of democracy is avoided.) What may be said, however, to be implied in the adoption of the democratic principle is the conviction that the acceptance of even a bad policy in a democracy (as long as we can work for a peaceful change) is preferable to the submission to a tyranny, however wise or benevolent. Seen in this light, the theory of democracy is not based upon the principle that the majority should rule; rather, the various equalitarian methods of democratic control, such as general elections and representative government, are to be considered as no more than well-tried and, in the presence of a widespread traditional distrust of tyranny, reasonably effective institutional safeguards against tyranny, always open to improvement, and even providing methods for their own improvement.

He who accepts the principle of democracy in this sense is not therefore bound to look upon the result of a democratic vote as an authoritative expression of what is right. Although he will accept a decision of the majority, for the sake of making the democratic institutions work, he will feel free to combat it by democratic means, and to work for its revision. And should he live to see the day when the majority vote destroys the democratic institutions, then this sad experience will tell him only that there does not exist a foolproof method of avoiding tyranny. But it need not weaken his decision to fight tyranny, nor will it expose his theory as inconsistent.

III

Returning to Plato, we find that by his emphasis upon the problem "who should rule," he implicitly assumed the general theory of sovereignty. The question of an institutional control of the rulers, and of an institutional balancing of their powers, is thereby eliminated without ever having been raised. The interest is shifted from institutions to questions of personnel, and the most urgent problem now becomes that of selecting the natural leaders, and that of training them for leadership.

In view of this fact some people think that in Plato's theory, the welfare of the state is ultimately an ethical and spiritual matter, depending on persons and personal responsibility rather than on the construction of impersonal institutions. I believe that this view of Platonism is superficial. *All long-term politics are institutional.* There is no escape from that, not even for Plato. The principle of leadership does not replace institutional problems by problems of personnel, it only creates new institutional problems. As we shall see, it even burdens the institutions with a task which goes beyond what can be reasonably demanded from a mere institution, namely, with *the task*

of selecting the future leaders. It would therefore be a mistake to
think that the opposition between the theory of balances and the
theory of sovereignty corresponds to that between institutionalism
and personalism. Plato's principle of leadership is far removed from
a pure personalism since it involves the working of institutions; and
indeed it may be said that a pure personalism is impossible. But it
must be said that a pure institutionalism is impossible also. Not only
does the construction of institutions involve important personal decisions, but the functioning of even the best institutions (such as
democratic checks and balances) will always depend, to a considerable degree, on the persons involved. Institutions are like fortresses.
They must be well designed *and* manned.

This distinction between the personal and the institutional element
in a social situation is a point which is often missed by the critics
of democracy. Most of them are dissatisfied with democratic institutions because they find that these do not necessarily prevent a state
or a policy from falling short of some moral standards or of some political demands which may be urgent as well as admirable. But these
critics misdirect their attacks; they do not understand what democratic institutions may be expected to do, and what the alternative
to democratic institutions would be. Democracy (using this label in
the sense suggested above) provides the institutional framework for
the reform of political institutions. It makes possible the reform of
institutions without using violence, and thereby the use of reason in
the designing of new institutions and the adjusting of old ones. It
cannot provide reason. The question of the intellectual and moral
standard of its citizens is to a large degree a personal problem. (The
idea that this problem can be tackled, in turn, by an institutional
eugenic and educational control is, I believe, mistaken; some reasons
for my belief will be given below.) It is quite wrong to blame democracy for the political shortcomings of a democratic state. We should
rather blame ourselves, that is to say, the citizens of the democratic
state. In a nondemocratic state, the only way to achieve reasonable
reforms is by the violent overthrow of the government, and the introduction of a democratic framework. Those who criticize democracy
on any "moral" grounds fail to distinguish between personal and
institutional problems. It rests with us to improve matters. The demo-

cratic institutions cannot improve themselves. The problem of improving them is always a problem for *persons* rather than for institutions. But if we want improvements, we must make clear which *institutions* we want to improve.

There is another distinction within the field of political problems corresponding to that between persons and institutions. It is the one between the problems of the day and the problems of the future. While the problems of the day are largely personal, the building of the future must necessarily be institutional. If the political problem is approached by asking "Who should rule," and if Plato's principle of leadership is adopted—that is to say, the principle that the best should rule—then the problem of the future must take the form of designing institutions for the selection of future leaders.

This is one of the most important problems in Plato's theory of education. In approaching it I do not hesitate to say that Plato utterly corrupted and confused the theory and practice of education by linking it up with his theory of leadership. The damage done is, if possible, even greater than that inflicted upon ethics by the identification of collectivism with altruism, and upon political theory by the introduction of the principle of sovereignty. Plato's assumption that it should be the task of education (or more precisely, of the educational institutions) to select the future leaders, and to train them for leadership, is still largely taken for granted. By burdening these institutions with a task which must go beyond the scope of any institution, Plato is partly responsible for their deplorable state. But before entering into a general discussion of his view of the task of education, I wish to develop, in more detail, his theory of leadership, the leadership of the wise.

IV

I think it most likely that this theory of Plato's owes a number of its elements to the influence of Socrates. One of the fundamental tenets of Socrates was, I believe, his moral intellectualism. By this I understand (*a*) his identification of goodness and wisdom, his theory that nobody acts against his better knowledge, and that lack of knowledge is responsible for all moral mistakes; (*b*) his theory that moral excellence can be taught, and that it does not presuppose any particular moral faculties, apart from the universal human intelligence.

Socrates was a moralist and an enthusiast. He was the type of man who would criticize any form of government for its shortcomings (and indeed, such criticism would be necessary and useful for any government, although it is possible only under a democracy) but he recognized the importance of being loyal to the laws of the state. As it happened, he spent his life largely under a democratic form of government, and as a good democrat he found it his duty to expose the incompetence and windbaggery of some of the democratic leaders of his time. At the same time, he opposed any form of tyranny; and if we consider his courageous behavior under the Thirty Tyrants then we have no reason to assume that his criticism of the democratic leaders was inspired by anything like antidemocratic leanings. It is not unlikely that he demanded (like Plato) that the best should rule, which would have meant, in his view, the wisest, or those who knew something about justice. But we must remember that by "justice" he meant equalitarian justice . . . and that he was not only an equalitarian but also an individualist—perhaps the greatest apostle of an individualistic ethics of all time. And we should realize that, if he demanded that the wisest men should rule, he clearly stressed that he did not mean the learned men; in fact, he was skeptical of all professional learnedness, whether it was that of the philosophers of the past or of the learned men of his own generation, the Sophists. The wisdom he meant was of a different kind. It was simply the realization: how little do I know! Those who did not know this, he taught, knew nothing at all. (This is the true scientific spirit. Some people still think, as Plato did when he had established himself as a learned Pythagorean sage, that Socrates' agnostic attitude must be explained by the lack of success of the science of his day. But this only shows that they do not understand this spirit, and that they are still possessed by the pre-Socratic magical attitude toward science, and toward the scientist, whom they consider as a somewhat glorified shaman, as wise, learned, initiated. They judge him by the amount of knowledge in his possession, instead of taking, with Socrates, his awareness of what he does not know as a measure of his scientific level as well as of his intellectual honesty.)

It is important to see that this Socratic intellectualism is decidedly equalitarian. Socrates believed that everyone can be taught; in the *Meno*, we see him teaching a young slave a version of the now so-called theorem of Pythagoras, in an attempt to prove that any uneducated slave has the capacity to grasp even abstract matters. And his intellectualism is also anti-authoritarian. A technique, for instance rhetoric, may perhaps be dogmatically taught by an expert, according to Socrates; but real knowledge, wisdom, and also virtue, can be taught only by a method which he describes as a form of midwifery. Those eager to learn may be helped to free themselves from their prejudice; thus they may learn self-criticism, and that truth is not easily attained. But they may also learn to make up their minds, and to rely, critically, on their decisions, and on their insight. In view of such teaching, it is clear how much the Socratic demand (if he ever raised this demand) that the best, i.e., the intellectually honest, should rule, differs from the authoritarian demand that the most learned, or from the aristocratic demand that the best, i.e., the most noble, should rule. (Socrates' belief that even courage is wisdom can, I think, be interpreted as a direct criticism of the aristocratic doctrine of the nobly born hero.)

But this moral intellectualism of Socrates is a two-edged sword. It has its equalitarian and democratic aspect, which was later developed by Antisthenes. But it has also an aspect which may give rise to strongly antidemocratic tendencies. Its stress upon the need for enlightenment, for education, might easily be misinterpreted as a demand for *authoritarianism*. This is connected with a question which seems to have puzzled Socrates a great deal: that those who are not sufficiently educated, and thus not wise enough to know their deficiencies, are just those who are in the greatest need of education. Readiness to learn in itself proves the possession of wisdom, in fact all the wisdom claimed by Socrates for himself; for he who is ready to learn knows how little he knows. The uneducated seems thus to be in need of an authority to wake him up, since he cannot be expected to be self-critical. But this one element of authoritarianism was wonderfully balanced in Socrates' teaching by the emphasis that the authority must not claim more than that. The true teacher can prove himself only by exhibiting that self-criticism which the uneducated lacks. "Whatever authority I may have rests solely upon my knowing how little I know": this is the way in which Socrates might have justified his mission to stir up the people from their dogmatic slumber. This educational mission he believed to be also a political mission. He felt that the way to improve the political life of the city was to educate the citizens to self-criticism. In this sense he claimed to be "the only politician of his day," in opposition to those others who flatter the people instead of furthering their true interests.

This Socratic identification of his educational and political activity could easily be distorted into the Platonic and Aristotelian demand that the state should look after the moral life of its citizens. And it can easily be used for a dangerously convincing proof that all democratic control is vicious. For how can those whose task it is to educate be judged by the uneducated? How can the better be controlled by the less good? But this argument is, of course, entirely un-Socratic. It assumes an authority of the wise and learned man, and goes far beyond Socrates' modest idea of the teacher's authority as founded solely on his consciousness of his own limitations. State-authority in these matters is liable to achieve, in fact, the exact opposite of Socrates' aim. It is liable to produce dogmatic self-satisfaction and massive intellectual complacency, instead of critical dissatisfaction and eagerness for improvement. I do not think that it is unnecessary to stress this danger which is seldom clearly realized. Even an author like Crossman, who, I believe, understood the true Socratic spirit, agrees with Plato in what he calls Plato's third criticism of Athens: "*Education, which should be the major responsibility of the State,* had been left to individual caprice. . . . Here again was a task which should be entrusted only to the man of proven probity. The future of any State depends on the younger generation, and it is therefore madness to allow the minds of children to be molded by individual taste and force of circumstances. Equally disastrous had been the State's *laissez-faire* policy with regard to teachers and schoolmasters and sophist-lecturers." But the Athenian state's *laissez-faire* policy, criticized by Crossman and Plato, had the invaluable result of enabling certain sophist-lecturers to teach, and especially the greatest of them all, Socrates. And when this policy was later dropped, the result was Socrates' death. This should be a warning that state control in such matters is dangerous, and that the cry for the "man of proven probity" may easily lead to the suppression of the best. (Bertrand

Russell's recent suppression is a case in point.) But as far as basic principles are concerned, we have here an instance of the deeply rooted prejudice that the only alternative to *laissez faire* is full state responsibility. I certainly believe that it is the responsibility of the state to see that its citizens are given an education enabling them to participate in the life of the community, and to make use of any opportunity to develop their special interests and gifts; and the state should certainly also see (as Crossman rightly stresses) that the lack of "the individual's capacity to pay" should not debar him from higher studies. This, I believe, belongs to the state's protective functions. To say, however, that "the future of the state depends on the younger generation, and that it is therefore madness to allow the minds of children to be molded by individual taste," appears to me to open wide the door to totalitarianism. State interest must not be lightly invoked to defend measures which may endanger the most precious of all forms of freedom, namely, intellectual freedom. And although I do not advocate "*laissez faire* with regard to teachers and schoolmasters," I believe that this policy is infinitely superior to an authoritative policy that gives officers of the state full powers to mold minds, and to control the teaching of science, thereby backing the dubious authority of the expert by that of the state, ruining science by the customary practice of teaching it as an authoritative doctrine, and destroying the scientific spirit of inquiry—the spirit of the search for truth, as opposed to the belief in its possession.

I have tried to show that Socrates' intellectualism was fundamentally equalitarian and individualistic, and that the element of authoritarianism which it involved was reduced to a minimum by Socrates' intellectual modesty and his scientific attitude. The intellectualism of Plato is very different from this. The Platonic "Socrates" of the *Republic* is the embodiment of an unmitigated authoritarianism. (Even his self-deprecating remarks are not based upon awareness of his limitations, but are rather an ironical way of asserting his superiority.) His educational aim is not the awakening of self-criticism and of critical thought in general. It is, rather, indoctrination—the molding of minds and of souls which (to repeat a quotation from the *Laws*) are "to become, by long habit, utterly incapable of doing anything at all independently." And Socrates' great equalitarian and liberating idea that it is possible to reason with a slave, and that there is an intel-

lectual link between man and man, a medium of universal understanding, namely, "reason," this idea is replaced by a demand for an
educational monopoly of the ruling class, coupled with the strictest
censorship, even of oral debates.

Socrates had stressed that he was not wise; that he was not in the
possession of truth, but that he was a searcher, an inquirer, a lover of
truth. This, he explained, is expressed by the word "philosopher,"
i.e., the lover of wisdom, and the seeker for it, as opposed to "Soph-
ist," i.e., the professionally wise man. If ever he claimed that statesmen should be philosophers, he could only have meant that, bur-
dened with an excessive responsibility, they should be searchers for
truth, and conscious of their limitations.

How did Plato convert this doctrine? At first sight, it might appear
that he did not alter it at all, when demanding that the sovereignty
of the state should be invested in the philosophers; especially since,
like Socrates, he defined philosophers as lovers of truth. But the
change made by Plato is indeed tremendous. His lover is no longer
the modest seeker, he is the proud possessor of truth. A trained
dialectician, he is capable of intellectual intuition, i.e., of seeing, and
of communicating with, the eternal, the heavenly Forms or Ideas.
Placed high above all ordinary men, he is "god like, if not . . . divine," both in his wisdom and in his power. Plato's ideal philosopher
approaches both to omniscience and to omnipotence. He is the Philosopher-King. It is hard, I think, to conceive a greater contrast than
that between the Socratic and the Platonic ideal of a philosopher. It
is the contrast between two worlds—the world of a modest, rational
individualist and that of a totalitarian demi-god.

Plato's demand that the wise man should rule—the possessor of
truth, the "fully qualified philosopher"—raises, of course, the problem of selecting and educating the rulers. In a purely personalist (as
opposed to an institutional) theory, this problem might be solved
simply by declaring that the wise ruler will in his wisdom be wise
enough to choose the best man for his successor. This is not, however, a very satisfactory approach to the problem. Too much would
depend on uncontrolled circumstances; an accident may destroy the
future stability of the state. But the attempt to control circumstances,
to foresee what might happen and to provide for it, must lead here,

as everywhere, to the abandonment of a purely personalist solution, and to its replacement by an institutional one. As already stated, the attempt to plan for the future must always lead to institutionalism.

V

The institution which according to Plato has to look after the future leaders can be described as the educational department of the state. It is, from a purely political point of view, by far the most important institution within Plato's society. It holds the keys to power. For this reason alone it should be clear that at least the higher grades of education are to be directly controlled by the rulers. But there are some additional reasons for this. The most important is that only "the expert and . . . the man of proven probity," as Crossman puts it, which in Plato's view means only the very wisest adepts, that is to say, the rulers themselves, can be entrusted with the final initiation of the future sages into the higher mysteries of wisdom. This holds, above all, for dialectics, i.e., the art of intellectual intuition, of visualizing the divine originals, the Forms or Ideas, of unveiling the Great Mystery behind the common man's everyday world of appearances.

What are Plato's institutional demands regarding this highest form of education? They are remarkable. He demands that only those who are past their prime of life should be admitted. "When their bodily strength begins to fail, and when they are past the age of public and military duties, then, and only then, should they be permitted to enter at will the sacred field . . . ," namely, the field of the highest dialectical studies. Plato's reason for this amazing rule is clear enough. He is afraid of the power of thought. "All great things are dangerous" is the remark by which he introduces the confession that he is afraid of the effect which philosophic thought may have upon brains which are not yet on the verge of old age. (All this he puts into the mouth of Socrates, who died in defense of his right of free discussion with the young.) But this is exactly what we should expect if we remember that Plato's fundamental aim was to arrest political change. In their youth, the members of the upper class shall fight. When they are too old to think independently, they shall become dogmatic students to be imbued with wisdom and authority in order to become sages themselves and to hand on their wisdom, the doctrine of collectivism and authoritarianism, to future generations.

It is interesting that in a later and more elaborate passage which attempts to paint the rulers in the brightest colors, Plato modifies his suggestion. Now he allows the future sages to begin their preparatory dialectical studies at the age of thirty, stressing, of course, "the need for great caution" and the dangers of "insubordination . . . which corrupts so many dialecticians"; and he demands that "those to whom the use of arguments may be permitted must possess disciplined and well-balanced natures." This alteration certainly helps to brighten the picture. But the fundamental tendency is the same. For, in the continuation of this passage, we hear that the future leaders must not be initiated into the higher philosophical studies—into the dialectic vision of the essence of the Good—before they reach, having passed through many tests and temptations, the age of fifty.

This is the teaching of the *Republic*. It seems that the dialogue *Parmenides* contains a similar message, for here Socrates is depicted as a brilliant young man who, having dabbled successfully in pure philosophy, gets into serious trouble when asked to give an account of the more subtle problems of the theory of ideas. He is dismissed by the old Parmenides with the admonition that he should train himself more thoroughly in the art of abstract thought before venturing again into the higher field of philosophical studies. It looks as if we had here (among other things) Plato's answer—"Even a Socrates was once too young for dialectics"—to his pupils who pestered him for an initiation which he considered premature.

Why is it that Plato does not wish his leaders to have originality or initiative? The reason, I think, is clear. He hates change and does not want to see that readjustments may become necessary. But this explanation of Plato's attitude does not go deep enough. In fact, we are faced here with a fundamental difficulty of the leader principle. The very idea of selecting or educating future leaders is self-contradictory. You may solve the problem, perhaps, to some degree in the field of bodily excellence. Physical initiative and bodily courage are perhaps not so hard to ascertain. But the secret of intellectual excellence is the spirit of criticism; it is intellectual independence. And this leads to difficulties which must prove insurmountable for any kind of authoritarianism. The authoritarian will in general select those who obey, who believe, who respond to his influence. But in doing so, he is bound to select mediocrities. For he excludes those who revolt, who doubt, who dare to resist his influence. Never can an authority admit that the intellectually courageous, i.e., those who dare to defy his authority, may be the most valuable type. Of course, the authorities will always remain convinced of their ability to detect initiative. But what they mean by this is only a quick grasp of their intentions, and they will remain forever incapable of seeing the difference. (Here we may perhaps penetrate the secret of the particular difficulty of selecting capable military leaders. The demands of military discipline enhance the difficulties discussed, and the methods of military advancement are such that those who do dare to think for themselves are usually eliminated. Nothing is less true, as far as intellectual initiative is concerned, than the idea that those who are good in obeying will also be good in commanding. Very similar difficulties arise in political parties: the "Man Friday" of the party leader is seldom a capable successor.)

We are led here, I believe, to a result of some importance, and to one which can be generalized. Institutions for the selection of the outstanding can hardly be devised. Institutional selection may work quite well for such purposes as Plato had in mind, namely for arresting change. But it will never work well if we demand more than that, for it will always tend to eliminate initiative and originality, and, more generally, qualities which are unusual and unexpected. This is not a criticism of political institutionalism. It only reaffirms what has been said before, that we should always prepare for the worst leaders, although we should try, of course, to get the best. But it *is* a criticism of the tendency to burden institutions, especially educational institutions, with the impossible task of selecting the best. This should never be made their task. This tendency transforms our educational system into a race-course, and turns a course of studies into a hurdle-race. Instead of encouraging the student to devote himself to his studies for the sake of studying, instead of encouraging in him a real love for his subject and for inquiry, he is encouraged to study for the sake of his personal career; he is led to acquire only such knowledge as is serviceable in getting him over the hurdles which he must clear for the sake of his advancement. In other words, even in the field of science, our methods of selection are based upon an appeal to personal ambition of a somewhat crude form. (It is a natural reaction to this appeal if the eager student is looked upon with suspicion by his colleagues.) The impossible demand for an institutional selection of intellectual leaders endangers the very life not only of science, but of intelligence.

It has been said, only too truly, that Plato was the inventor of both our secondary schools and our universities. I do not know a better argument for an optimistic view of mankind, no better proof of their indestructible love for truth and decency, of their originality and stubbornness and health, than the fact that this devastating system of education has not utterly ruined them. In spite of the treachery of so many of their leaders, there are quite a number, old as well as young, who are decent, and intelligent, and devoted to their task. "I sometimes wonder how it was that the mischief done was not more clearly perceptible," says Samuel Butler, "and that the young men and women grew up as sensible and goodly as they did, in spite of the attempts almost deliberately made to warp and stunt their growth. Some doubtless received damage, from which they suffered to their life's end; but many seemed little or none the worse, and some almost the better. The reason would seem to be that the natural instinct of the lads in most cases so absolutely rebelled against their training, that do what the teachers might they could never get them to pay serious heed to it."

It may be mentioned here that, in practice, Plato did not prove too successful as a selector of political leaders. I have in mind not so much the disappointing outcome of his experiment with Dionysius the Younger, tyrant of Syracuse, but rather the participation of Plato's Academy in Dion's successful expedition against Dionysius. Plato's famous friend Dion was supported in this adventure by a number of members of Plato's Academy. One of them was Callippus, who became Dion's most trusted comrade. After Dion had made himself tyrant of Syracuse he ordered Heraclides, his ally (and perhaps his rival), to be murdered. Shortly afterwards he was himself murdered by Callippus who usurped the tyranny, which he lost after thirteen months. (He was, in turn, murdered by the Pythagorean philosopher Leptines.) But this event was not the only one of its kind in Plato's career as a teacher. Clearchus, one of Plato's (and of Isocrates') disciples, made himself tyrant of Heraclea after having posed as a democratic leader. He was murdered by his relation, Chion, another member of Plato's Academy. (We cannot know how Chion, whom some represent as an idealist, would have developed, since he was soon killed.) These and a few similar experiences of Plato's—who could boast a total of at least nine tyrants among his one-time pupils and associates—throw light on the peculiar difficulties connected with the selection of men who are to be invested with absolute power. It is hard to find a man whose character will not be corrupted by it. As Lord Acton says—all power corrupts, and absolute power corrupts absolutely.

To sum up. Plato's political program was much more institutional than personalist; he hoped to arrest political change by the institutional control of succession in leadership. The control was to be educational, based upon an authoritarian view of learning—upon the authority of the learned expert, and "the man of proven probity." This is what Plato made of Socrates' demand that a responsible politician should be a lover of truth and of wisdom rather than an expert, and that he was wise only if he knew his limitations.

The philosopher-king

The contrast between the Platonic and the Socratic creed is even greater than I have shown so far. Plato, I have said, followed Socrates in his definition of the philosopher. "Whom do you call true philosophers?—Those who love truth," we read in the *Republic*. But he himself is not quite truthful when he makes this statement. He does not really believe in it, for he bluntly declares in other places that it is one of the royal privileges of the sovereign to make full use of lies and deceit: "It is the business of the rulers of the city, if it is anybody's, to tell lies, deceiving both its enemies and its own citizens for the benefit of the city; and no one else must touch this privilege."

"For the benefit of the city," says Plato. Again we find that the appeal to the principle of collective utility is the ultimate ethical consideration. Totalitarian morality overrules everything, even the definition, the Idea, of the philosopher. It need hardly be mentioned that, by the same principle of political expediency, the ruled are to be forced to tell the truth. "If the ruler catches *anyone else* in a lie . . .

then he will punish him for introducing a practice which injures and endangers the city. . . ." Only in this slightly unexpected sense are the Platonic rulers—the philosopher-kings—lovers of truth.

I

Plato illustrates this application of his principle of collective utility to the problem of truthfulness by the example of the physician. The example is well chosen, since Plato likes to visualize his political mission as one of the healer or savior of the sick body of society. Apart from this, the role which he assigns to medicine throws light upon the totalitarian character of Plato's city where state interest dominates the life of the citizen from the mating of his parents to his grave. Plato interprets medicine as a form of politics, or as he puts it himself, he "regards Aesculapius, the god of medicine, as a politician." Medical art, he explains, must not consider the prolongation of life as its aim, but only the interest of the state. "In all properly ruled communities, each man has his particular work assigned to him in the state. This he must do, and no one has time to spend his life in falling ill and getting cured." Accordingly, the physician has "no right to attend to a man who cannot carry out his ordinary duties; for such a man is useless to himself and to the state." To this is added the consideration that such a man might have "children who would probably be equally sick," and who also would become a burden to the state. (In his old age, Plato mentions medicine, in spite of his increased hatred of individualism, in a more personal vein. He complains of the doctor who treats even free citizens as if they were slaves, "issuing his orders like a tyrant whose will is law, and then rushing off to the next slave-patient," and he pleads for more gentleness and patience in medical treatment, at least for those who are not slaves.) Concerning the use of lies and deceit, Plato urges that these are "useful only as a medicine"; but the ruler of the state, Plato insists, must not behave like some of those "ordinary doctors" who have not the courage to administer strong medicines. The philosopher king, a lover of truth as a philosopher, must, as a king, be "a more courageous man," since he must be determined "to administer a great many lies and deceptions"—for the benefit of the ruled, Plato hastens to add. Which means, as we already know, and as we learn here again from

Plato's reference to medicine, "for the benefit of the state." (Kant remarked once in a very different spirit that the sentence "Truthfulness is the best policy" might indeed be questionable, whilst the sentence "Truthfulness is better than policy" is beyond dispute.)

What kind of lies has Plato in mind when he exhorts his rulers to use strong medicine? Crossman rightly emphasizes that Plato means "propaganda, the technique of controlling the behavior of . . . the bulk of the ruled majority." Certainly, Plato had these first in his mind; but when Crossman suggests that the propaganda lies were only intended for the consumption of the ruled, while the rulers should be a fully enlightened intelligentsia, then I cannot agree. I think, rather, that Plato's complete break with anything resembling Socrates' intellectualism is nowhere more obvious than in the place where he twice expresses his hope that even *the rulers themselves*, at least after a few generations, might be induced to believe his greatest propaganda lie; I mean his racialism, his Myth of Blood and Soil, known as the Myth of the Metals in Man and of the Earthborn. Here we see that Plato's utilitarian and totalitarian principles overrule everything, even the ruler's privilege of knowing, and of demanding to be told, the truth. The motive of Plato's wish that the rulers themselves should believe in the propaganda lie is his hope of increasing its wholesome effect, i.e., of strengthening the rule of the master race and, ultimately, of arresting all political change.

II

Plato introduces his Myth of Blood and Soil with the blunt admission that it is a fraud. "Well then," says the Socrates of the *Republic*, "could we perhaps fabricate one of those very handy lies which indeed we mentioned just recently? With the help of one single lordly lie we may, if we are lucky, persuade even the rulers themselves—but at any rate the rest of the city." It is interesting to note the use of the term "persuade." To persuade somebody to believe a lie means, more precisely, to mislead or to hoax him; and it would be more in tune with the frank cynicism of the passage to translate "we may, if we are lucky, hoax even the rulers themselves." But Plato uses the term "persuasion" very frequently, and its occurrence here throws some light on other passages. It may be taken as a warning that in similar passages he may have propaganda lies in his mind; more especially where he advocates that the statesman should rule "by means of both persuasion and force."

After announcing his "lordly lie," Plato, instead of proceeding directly to the narration of his Myth, first develops a lengthy preface, somewhat similar to the lengthy preface which precedes his discovery of justice; an indication, I think, of his uneasiness. It seems that he did not expect the proposal which follows to find much favor with his readers. The Myth itself introduces two ideas. The first is to strengthen the defense of the mother country; it is the idea that the warriors of his city are autochthonous, "born of the earth of their country," and ready to defend their country which is their mother. This old and well-known idea is certainly not the reason for Plato's hesitation (although the wording of the dialogue cleverly suggests it). The second idea, however, "the rest of the story," is the myth of racialism: "God . . . has put gold into those who are capable of ruling, silver into the auxiliaries, and iron and copper into the peasants and the other producing classes." These metals are hereditary, they are racial characteristics. In this passage, in which Plato, hesitatingly, first introduces his racialism, he allows for the possibility that children may be born with an admixture of another metal than those of their parents; and it must be admitted that he here announces the following rule: if in one of the lower classes "children are born with an admixture of gold and silver, they shall . . . be appointed guardians, and . . . auxiliaries." But this concession is rescinded in later passages of the *Republic* (and also in the *Laws*), especially in the story of the Fall of Man and of the Number. . . . From this passage we learn that *any* admixture of one of the base metals must be excluded from the higher classes. The possibility of admixtures and corresponding changes in status therefore only means that nobly born but degenerate children may be pushed down, and not that any of the base born may be lifted up. The way in which any mixing of metals must lead to destruction is described in the concluding passage of the story of the Fall of Man: "Iron will mingle with silver and bronze with gold, and from this mixture variation will be born and absurd irregularity; and whenever these are born they will beget struggle and hostility. And this is how we must describe the ancestry and birth of Dissension, wherever she arises." It is in this light that we must consider that the Myth of the Earthborn concludes with the cynical fabrication of a prophecy by a fictitious oracle 'that the city must perish when guarded by iron and copper. Plato's reluctance to proffer his racialism at once in its more radical form indicates, I suppose, that he knew how much it was opposed to the democratic and humanitarian tendencies of his time.

If we consider Plato's blunt admission that his Myth of Blood and Soil is a propaganda lie, then the attitude of the commentators toward the Myth is somewhat puzzling. Adam, for instance, writes: "Without it, the present sketch of a state would be incomplete. We require some guarantee for the permanence of the city . . . ; and nothing could be more in keeping with the *prevailing moral and religious spirit* of Plato's . . . education than that he should find that guarantee in *faith rather than in reason*." I agree (though this is not quite what Adam meant) that nothing is more in keeping with Plato's totalitarian morality than his advocacy of propaganda lies. But I do not quite understand how the religious and idealistic commentator can declare, by implication, that religion and faith are on the level of an opportunist lie. As a matter of fact, Adam's comment is reminiscent of Hobbes' conventionalism, of the view that the tenets of religion, although not true, are a most expedient and indispensable political device. And this consideration shows us that Plato, after all, was more of a conventionalist than one might think. He does not even stop short of establishing a religious faith "by convention" (we must credit him with the frankness of his admission that it is only a fabrication), while the reputed conventionalist Protagoras at least believed that the laws, which are our making, are made with the help of divine inspiration. It is hard to understand why those of Plato's commentators who praise him for fighting against the subversive conventionalism of the Sophists, and for establishing a spiritual naturalism ultimately based on religion, fail to censure him for making a convention, or rather an invention, the ultimate basis of religion. In fact, Plato's attitude toward religion as revealed by his "lordly lie" is almost identical with that of Critias, his beloved uncle, the brilliant leader of the Thirty Tyrants who established an inglorious blood-regime in Athens after the Peloponnesian war. Critias, a poet, was the first to glorify propaganda lies, whose invention he described in forceful verses eulogizing the wise and cunning man who fabricated religion, in order to "persuade" the people, i.e., to threaten them into submission.

> Then came, it seems, that wise and cunning man,
> The first inventor of the fear of god. . . .
> He framed a tale, a most alluring doctrine,
> Concealing truth by veils of lying lore.
> He told of the abode of awful gods,
> Up in revolving vaults, whence thunder roars
> And lightning's fearful flashes blind the eye. . . .
> He thus encircled men by bonds of fear;
> Surrounding them by gods in fair abodes,
> He charmed them by his spells, and daunted them—
> And lawlessness turned into law and order.

In Critias' view, religion is nothing but the lordly lie of a great and clever statesman. Plato's views are strikingly similar, both in the introduction of the Myth in the *Republic* (where he bluntly admits that the Myth is a lie) and in the *Laws* where he says that the installation of rites and of gods is "a matter for a great thinker."—But is this the whole truth about Plato's religious attitude? Was Plato an opportunist *only* in these matters, and was the very different spirit of his earlier works merely Socratic? There is, of course, no way of deciding this question with certainty, though I feel, intuitively, that there may sometimes be a more genuine religious feeling expressed even in the latter works. But I believe that wherever Plato considers religious matters in their relation to politics, his political opportunism sweeps all other feelings aside. Thus Plato demands, in the *Laws*, the severest punishment even for honest and honorable people if their opinions concerning the gods deviate from those held by the state. Their souls are to be treated by a Nocturnal Council of inquisitors, and if they do not recant or if they repeat the offense, the charge of impiety means death. Has he forgotten that Socrates had fallen a victim to that very charge?

That it is mainly state interest which inspires these demands, rather than interest in the religious faith as such, can be gauged by Plato's central religious doctrine. The gods, he teaches in the *Laws*, punish

severely all those on the wrong side in the conflict between good
and evil, a conflict which is explained as that between collectivism
and individualism. And the gods, he insists, take an active interest in
men, they are not merely spectators. It is impossible to appease them.
Neither through prayers nor through sacrifices can they be moved to
abstain from punishment. The political interest behind this teaching
is clear, and it is made even clearer by Plato's demand that the state
must suppress all doubt about any part of this politico-religious
dogma, and especially about the doctrine that the gods never abstain
from punishment.

Plato's opportunism and his theory of lies makes it, of course,
difficult to interpret what he says. How far did he believe in his theory
of justice? How far did he believe in the truth of the religious doctrines he preached? Was he perhaps himself an atheist, in spite of
his demand for the punishment of other (lesser) atheists? Although
we cannot hope to answer any of these questions definitely, it is,
I believe, difficult, and methodologically unsound, not to give Plato
at least the benefit of the doubt. And especially the fundamental
sincerity of his belief that there is an urgent need to arrest all change
can, I think, hardly be questioned. . . . On the other hand, we
cannot doubt that Plato subjects the Socratic love of truth to the
more fundamental principle that the rule of the master class must be
strengthened.

It is interesting, however, to note that Plato's theory of truth is
slightly less radical than his theory of justice. Justice, we have seen,
is defined, practically, as that which serves the interest of his totalitarian state. It would have been possible, of course, to define the
concept of truth in the same utilitarian or pragmatist fashion. The
Myth is true, Plato could have said, since anything that serves the
interest of my state must be believed and therefore must be called
"true"; and there must be no other criterion of truth. In theory, an
analogous step has actually been taken by the pragmatist successors
of Hegel; in practice, it has been taken by Hegel himself and his
racialist successors. But Plato retained enough of the Socratic spirit
to admit candidly that he was lying. The step taken by the school of
Hegel was one that could never have occurred, I think, to any
companion of Socrates.

III

So much for the role played by the Idea of Truth in Plato's best state. But apart from Justice and Truth, we have still to consider some further Ideas, such as Goodness, Beauty, and Happiness, if we wish to remove the objections . . . against our interpretation of Plato's political program as purely totalitarian, and as based on historicism. An approach to the discussion of these Ideas, and also to that of Wisdom, which has been partly discussed in the previous chapter, can be made by considering the somewhat negative result reached by our discussion of the Idea of Truth. For this result raises a new problem: Why does Plato demand that the philosophers should be kings or the kings philosophers, if he defines the philosopher as a lover of truth, insisting, on the other hand, that the king must be "more courageous," and use lies?

The only reply to this question is, of course, that Plato has, in fact, something very different in mind when he uses the term "philosopher." And indeed, we have seen in the last chapter that his philosopher is not the devoted seeker for wisdom, but its proud possessor. He is a learned man, a sage. What Plato demands, therefore, is the rule of learnedness—*sophocracy*, if I may say so. In order to understand this demand, we must try to find what kind of functions make it desirable that the ruler of Plato's state should be a possessor of knowledge, a "fully qualified philosopher," as Plato says. The functions to be considered can be divided into two main groups, namely those connected with the *foundation* of the state, and those connected with its *preservation*.

IV

The first and the most important function of the philosopher king is that of the city's founder and lawgiver. It is clear why Plato needs a philosopher for this task. If the state is to be stable, then it must be a true copy of the divine Form or Idea of the State. But only a philosopher who is fully proficient in the highest of sciences, in dialectics, is able to see, and to copy, the heavenly Original. This point receives much emphasis in the part of the *Republic* in which

Plato develops his arguments for the sovereignty of the philosophers. Philosophers "love to see the truth," and a real lover always loves to see the whole, not merely the parts. Thus he does not love, as ordinary people do, sensible things and their "beautiful sounds and colors and shapes," but he wants "to see, and to admire the real nature of beauty"—the Form or Idea of Beauty. *In this way, Plato gives the term philosopher a new meaning*, that of a lover and a seer of the divine world of Forms or Ideas. As such, the philosopher is the man who may become the founder of a virtuous city: "The philosopher who has communion with the divine" may be "overwhelmed by the urge to realize . . . his heavenly vision," of the ideal city and of its ideal citizens. He is like a draughtsman or a painter who has "the divine as his model." Only true philosophers can "sketch the ground-plan of the city," for they alone can see the original, and can copy it, by "letting their eyes wander to and fro, from the model to the picture, and back from the picture to the model."

As "a painter of constitutions," the philosopher must be helped by the light of goodness and of wisdom. A few remarks will be added concerning these two ideas, and their significance for the philosopher in his function as a founder of the city.

Plato's *Idea of the Good* is the highest in the hierarchy of Forms. It is the sun of the divine world of Forms or Ideas, which not only sheds light on all the other members, but is the source of their existence. It is also the source or cause of all knowledge and all truth. The power of seeing, of appreciating, of knowing the Good is thus indispensable to the dialectician. Since it is the sun and the source of light in the world of Forms, it enables the philosopher-painter to discern his objects. Its function is therefore of the greatest importance for the founder of the city. But this purely formal information is all we get. Plato's Idea of the Good nowhere plays a more direct ethical or political role; never do we hear which deeds are good, or produce good, apart from the well-known collectivist moral code whose precepts are introduced without recourse to the Idea of the Good. Remarks that the Good is the aim, that it is desired by every man, do not enrich our information. This empty formalism is still more marked in the *Philebus*, where the Good is identified with the Idea of "measure" or "mean." And when I read the report that Plato, in his famous lecture "On the Good," disappointed an uneducated audience by defining the Good as "the class of the determinate conceived as a unity," then my sympathy is with the audience. In the *Republic*, Plato says frankly that he cannot explain what he means by "the Good." The only practical suggestion we ever get is . . . that good is everything that preserves, and evil everything that leads to corruption or degeneration. ("Good" does not, however, seem to be here the Idea of the Good, but rather a property of things which makes them resemble the ideas.) Good is, accordingly, an unchanging, an arrested state of things; it is the state of things at rest.

This does not seem to carry us very far beyond Plato's political totalitarianism; and the analysis of Plato's *Idea of Wisdom* leads to equally disappointing results. Wisdom, as we have seen, does not mean to Plato the Socratic insight into one's own limitations; nor does it mean what most of us would expect, a warm interest in, and a helpful understanding of, humanity and human affairs. Plato's wise men, highly preoccupied with the problems of a superior world, "have no time to look down at the affairs of men . . . ; they look upon, and hold fast to, the ordered and the measured." It is the right kind of learning that makes a man wise: "Philosophic natures are lovers of that kind of learning which reveals to them a reality that exists for ever and does not stray toward generation and degeneration." It does not seem that Plato's treatment of wisdom can carry us beyond the ideal of arresting change.

V

Although the analysis of the functions of the city's founder has not revealed any new ethical elements in Plato's doctrine, it has shown that there is a definite reason why the founder of the city must be a philosopher. But this does not fully justify the demand for the permanent sovereignty of the philosopher. It only explains why the philosopher must be the first lawgiver, but not why he is needed as the permanent ruler, especially since none of the later rulers must introduce any change. For a full justification of the demand that the philosophers should rule, we must therefore proceed to analyze the tasks connected with the city's preservation.

We know from Plato's sociological theories that the state, once established, will continue to be stable as long as there is no split in the unity of the master class. The bringing up of that class is, therefore, the great preserving function of the sovereign, and a function which must continue as long as the state exists. How far does it justify the demand that a philosopher must rule? To answer this question, we distinguish again, within this function, between two different activities: the supervision of education, and the supervision of eugenic breeding.

Why should the director of education be a philosopher? Why is it not sufficient, once the state and its educational system are established, to put an experienced general, a soldier-king, in charge of it? The answer that the educational system must provide not only soldiers but philosophers, and therefore needs philosophers as well as soldiers as supervisors, is obviously unsatisfactory; for if no philosophers were needed as directors of education and as permanent rulers, then there would be no need for the educational system to produce new ones. The requirements of the educational system cannot as such justify the need for philosophers in Plato's state, or the postulate that the rulers must be philosophers. This would be different, of course, if Plato's education had an individualistic aim, apart from its aim to serve the interest of the state; for example, the aim to develop philosophical faculties for their own sake. But when we see, as we did in the preceding chapter, how frightened Plato was of permitting anything like independent thought; and when we now see that the ultimate theoretical aim of this philosophic education was merely a "Knowledge of the Idea of the Good" which is incapable of giving an articulate account of this Idea, then we begin to realize that this cannot be the explanation. . . . The great importance which Plato attaches to a philosophical education of the rulers must be explained by other reasons—by reasons which must be purely political.

The main reason I can see is the need for increasing to the utmost the authority of the rulers. If the education of the auxiliaries functions properly, there will be plenty of good soldiers. Outstanding military faculties may therefore be insufficient to establish an unchallenged and unchallengeable authority. This must be based on higher claims. Plato bases it upon the claims of supernatural, mystical powers which he develops in his leaders. They are not like other men. They belong to another world, they communicate with the divine.

Thus the philosopher king seems to be, partly, a copy of a tribal priest-king. . . . (The institution of tribal priest-kings or medicine-men or shamans seems also to have influenced the old Pythagorean sect, with their amazingly naïve tribal taboos. Apparently, most of these were dropped even before Plato. But the claim of the Pythagoreans to a supernatural basis of their authority remained.) Thus Plato's philosophical education has a definite political function. *It puts a mark on the rulers, and it establishes a barrier between the rulers and the ruled.* (This has remained a major function of "higher" education down to our own time.) Platonic wisdom is acquired largely for the sake of establishing a permanent political class rule. It can be described as political "medicine," giving mystic powers to its possessors, the medicine-men.

But this cannot be the full answer to our question of the functions of the philosopher in the state. It means, rather, that the question why a philosopher is needed has only been shifted, and that we would have now to raise the analogous question of the practical political functions of the shaman or the medicine-man. Plato must have had some definite aim when he devised his specialized philosophic training. We must look for a permanent function of the ruler, analogous to the temporary function of the lawgiver. The only hope of discovering such a function seems to be in the field of breeding the master race.

VI

The best way to find out why a philosopher is needed as a permanent ruler is to ask the question: What happens, according to Plato, to a state which is not permanently ruled by a philosopher? Plato has given a clear answer to this question. If the guardians of the state, even of a very perfect one, are unaware of Pythagorean lore and of the Platonic Number, then the race of the guardians, and with it the state, must degenerate.

Racialism thus takes up a more central part in Plato's political program than one would expect at first sight. Just as the Platonic racial or nuptial Number provides the setting for his descriptive sociology, "the setting in which Plato's Philosophy of History is framed" (as Adam puts it), so it also provides the setting of Plato's political demand for the sovereignty of the philosophers. . . . The need for scientific, for mathematico-dialectical and philosophical breeding is not the least of the arguments behind the claim for the sovereignty of the philosophers.

. . . The problem of obtaining a pure breed of human watch-dogs is emphasized and elaborated in the earlier parts of the *Republic*. But so far we have not met with any plausible reason why only a genuine and fully qualified philosopher should be a proficient and successful political breeder. And yet, as every breeder of dogs or horses or birds knows, rational breeding is impossible without a pattern, an aim to guide him in his efforts, an ideal which he may try to approach by the methods of mating and of selecting. Without such a standard, he could never decide which offspring is "good enough"; he could never speak of the difference between "good offspring" and "bad offspring." But this standard corresponds exactly to a Platonic Idea of the race which he intends to breed.

Just as only the true philosopher, the dialectician, can see, according to Plato, the divine original of the city, so it is only the dialectician who can see that other divine original—the Form or Idea of Man. Only he is capable of copying this model, of calling it down from Heaven to Earth, and of realizing it here. It is a kingly Idea, this Idea of Man. It does not, as some have thought, represent what is common to all men; it is not the universal concept "man." It is, rather, the godlike original of man, an unchanging superman; it is a super-Greek, and a super-master. The philosopher must try to realize on earth what Plato describes as the race of "the most constant, the most virile, and, within the limits of possibilities, the most beautifully formed men . . . ; nobly born, and of awe-inspiring character." It is to be a race of men and women who are "godlike if not divine . . . sculptured in perfect beauty"—a lordly race, destined by nature to kingship and mastery.

We see that the two fundamental functions of the philosopher-king are analogous: he has to copy the divine original of the city, and he has to copy the divine original of man. He is the only one who is able, and who has the urge, "to realize, in the individual as well as in the city, his heavenly vision."

Now we can understand why Plato drops his first hint that a more than ordinary excellence is needed in his rulers in the same place where he first claims that the principles of animal breeding must be applied to the race of men. We are, he says, most careful in breeding animals. "If you did not breed them in this way, don't you think that the race of your birds or your dogs would quickly degenerate?" When inferring from this that man must be bred in the same careful way, "Socrates" exclaims: "Good heavens! . . . What surpassing excellence we shall have to demand from our rulers, if the same principles apply to the race of men!" This exclamation is significant; it is one of the first hints that the rulers may constitute a class of "surpassing excellence" with status and training of their own; and it thus prepares us for the demand that they ought to be philosophers. But the passage is even more significant insofar as it directly leads to Plato's demand that it must be the duty of the rulers, as doctors of the race of men, to administer lies and deception. Lies are necessary, Plato asserts, "if your herd is to reach highest perfection"; for this needs "arrangements that must be kept secret from all but the rulers, if we wish to keep the herd of guardians really free from disunion." Indeed, the appeal (quoted above) to the rulers for more courage in administering lies as a medicine is made in this connection; it prepares the reader for the next demand, considered by Plato as particularly important. He decrees that the rulers should fabricate, for the purpose of mating the young auxiliaries, "an ingenious system of balloting, so that the persons who have been disappointed . . . may blame their bad luck, and not the rulers," who are, secretly, to engineer the ballot. And immediately after this despicable advice for dodging the admission of responsibility (by putting it into the mouth of Socrates, Plato libels his great teacher), "Socrates" makes a suggestion which is soon taken up and elaborated by Glaucon and which we may therefore call the *Glauconic Edict*. I mean the brutal law which imposes on everybody of either sex the duty of submitting, for the duration of a war, to the wishes of the brave: "As long as the war lasts . . . nobody may say 'No' to him. Accordingly, if a soldier wishes to make love to anybody, whether male or female, this law will make him more eager to carry off the price of valor." The state, it is carefully pointed out, will thereby obtain two distinct benefits— more heroes, owing to the incitement, and again more heroes, owing to the increased numbers of children from heroes. (The latter benefit, as the most important one from the point of view of a long-term racial policy, is put into the mouth of "Socrates.")

VII

No special philosophical training is required for this kind of breeding. Philosophical breeding, however, plays its main part in counteracting the dangers of degeneration. In order to fight these dangers, a fully qualified philosopher is needed, i.e., one who is trained in pure mathematics (including solid geometry), pure astronomy, pure harmonics, and, the crowning achievement of all, in dialectics. Only he who knows the secrets of mathematical eugenics, of the Platonic Number, can bring back to man, and preserve for him, the happiness enjoyed before the Fall. All this should be borne in mind when, after the announcement of the Glauconic Edict (and after an interlude dealing with the natural distinction between Greeks and Barbarians, corresponding, according to Plato, to that between masters and slaves), the doctrine is enunciated which Plato carefully marks as his central and most sensational political demand—the sovereignty of the philosopher-king. This demand alone, he teaches, can put an end to the evils of social life; to the evil rampant in states, i.e., *political instability*, as well as to its more hidden cause, the evil rampant in the members of the race of men, i.e., *racial degeneration*. This is the passage.

"Well," says Socrates, "I am now about to dive into that topic which I compared before to the greatest wave of all. Yet I must speak, even though I foresee that this will bring upon me a deluge of laughter. Indeed, I can see it now, this very wave, breaking over my head into an uproar of laughter and defamation . . ."—"Out with the story!" says Glaucon. "Unless," says Socrates, "unless, in their cities, philosophers are vested with the might of kings, or those now called kings and oligarchs become genuine and fully qualified philosophers; and unless these two, political might and philosophy, are fused (while the many who nowadays follow their natural inclination for only one of these two are suppressed by force), unless this happens, my dear Glaucon, there can be no rest; and the evil will not cease to be rampant in the cities—nor, I believe, in the race of men."

(To which Kant wisely replied: "That kings should become philosophers, or philosophers kings, is not likely to happen; nor would it be
desirable, since the possession of power invariably debases the free
judgment of reason. It is, however, indispensable that a king—or a
kingly, i.e., self-ruling, people—should *not suppress* philosophers but
leave them the right of public utterance.")

This important Platonic passage has been quite appropriately described as the key to the whole work. Its last words, "nor, I believe,
in the race of men," are, I think, an afterthought of comparatively
minor importance in this place. It is, however, necessary to comment
upon them, since the habit of idealizing Plato has led to the interpretation that Plato speaks here about "humanity," extending his
promise of salvation from the scope of the cities to that of "mankind
as a whole." It must be said, in this connection, that the ethical
category of "humanity" as something that transcends the distinction
of nations, races, and classes, is entirely foreign to Plato. In fact, we
have sufficient evidence of Plato's hostility towards the equalitarian
creed, a hostility which is seen in his attitude towards Antisthenes,
an old disciple and friend of Socrates. Antisthenes also belonged to
the school of Gorgias, like Alcidamas and Lycophron, whose equalitarian theories he seems to have extended into the doctrine of the
brotherhood of all men, and of the universal empire of men. This
creed is attacked in the Republic by correlating the natural inequality
of Greeks and Barbarians to that of masters and slaves; and it so
happens that this attack is launched immediately before the key
passage we are here considering. For these and other reasons, it seems
safe to assume that Plato, when speaking of the evil rampant in the
race of men, alluded to a theory with which his readers would be
sufficiently acquainted at this place, namely, to his theory that the
welfare of the state depends, ultimately, upon the "nature" of the
individual members of the ruling class; and that their nature, and the
nature of their race, or offspring, is threatened, in turn, by the evils of
an individualistic education, and, more important still, by racial degeneration. Plato's remark, with its clear allusion to the opposition
between divine rest and the evil of change and decay, foreshadows
the story of the Number and the Fall of Man.

It is very appropriate that Plato should allude to his racialism in
this key passage in which he enunciates his most important political

demand. For without the "genuine and fully qualified philosopher," trained in all those sciences which are prerequisite to eugenics, the state is lost. In his story of the Number and the Fall of Man, Plato tells us that one of the first and fatal sins of omission committed by the degenerate guardians will be their loss of interest in eugenics, in watching and testing the purity of the race: "Hence rulers will be ordained who are altogether unfit for their task as guardians; namely, to watch, and to test, the metals in the races (which are Hesiod's races as well as yours), gold and silver and bronze and iron."

It is ignorance of the mysterious nuptial Number which leads to all that. But the Number was undoubtedly Plato's own invention. (It presupposes pure harmonics, which in turn presupposes solid geometry, a new science at the time when the *Republic* was written.) Thus we see that nobody but Plato himself knew the secret of, and held the key to, true guardianship. But this can mean only one thing. The philosopher-king is Plato himself, and the *Republic* is Plato's own claim for kingly power—to the power which he thought his due, uniting in himself, as he did, both the claims of the philosopher and of the descendant and legitimate heir of Codrus the martyr, the last of Athens' kings, who, according to Plato, had sacrificed himself "in order to preserve the kingdom for his children."

VIII

Once this conclusion has been reached, many things which otherwise would remain unrelated become connected and clear. It can hardly be doubted, for instance, that Plato's work, full of allusions as it is to contemporary problems and characters, was meant by its author not so much as a theoretical treatise, but as a topical political manifesto. "We do Plato the gravest of wrongs," says A. E. Taylor, "if we forget that the *Republic* is no mere collection of theoretical discussions about government . . . but a serious project of practical reform put forward by an Athenian . . . set on fire, like Shelley, with a 'passion for reforming the world.'" This is undoubtedly true, and we could have concluded from this consideration alone that, in describing his philosopher-kings, Plato must have thought of some of the contemporary philosophers. But in the days when the *Republic* was written, there were in Athens only three outstanding men who might have claimed to be philosophers: Antisthenes, Isocrates, and Plato himself. If we approach the *Republic* with this in mind, we find at once that, in the discussion of the characteristics of the philosopher-kings, there is a lengthy passage which is clearly marked out by Plato as containing personal allusions. It begins with an unmistakable allusion to a popular character, namely Alcibiades, and ends by openly mentioning a name (that of Theages), and with a reference of "Socrates" to himself. Its upshot is that only very few can be described as true philosophers, eligible for the post of philosopher king. The nobly born Alcibiades, who was of the right type, deserted philosophy, in spite of Socrates' attempts to save him. Deserted and defenseless, philosophy was claimed by unworthy suitors. Ultimately, "there is left only a handful of men who are worthy of being associated with philosophy." From the point of view we have reached, we would have to expect that the "unworthy suitors" are Antisthenes and Isocrates and their school (and that they are the same people whom Plato demands to have "suppressed by force," as he says in the key-passage of the philosopher-king). And, indeed, there is some independent evidence corroborating this expectation. Similarly, we should expect that the "handful of men who are worthy" includes Plato and, perhaps, some of his friends (possibly Dion); and, indeed, a continuation of this passage leaves little doubt that Plato speaks here of himself: "He who belongs to this small band . . . can see the madness of the many, and the general corruption of all public affairs. The philosopher . . . is like a man in a cage of wild beasts. He will not share the injustice of the many, but his power does not suffice for continuing his fight alone, surrounded as he is by a world of savages. He would be killed before he could do any good, to his city or to his friends. . . . Having duly considered all these points, he will hold his peace, and confine his efforts to his own work. . . ." The strong resentment expressed in these sour and most un-Socratic words marks them clearly as Plato's own. For a full appreciation, however, of this personal confession, it must be compared with the following: "It is not in accordance with nature that the skilled navigator should beg the unskilled sailors to accept his command; nor that the wise man should wait at the doors of the rich. . . . But the true and natural procedure is that the sick, whether rich or poor, should hasten to the doctor's door. Likewise should those who need to be ruled besiege the door of him who can rule; and never should a ruler beg them to accept his rule, if he is any good at all." Who can miss the sound of an immense personal pride in this passage? Here am I, says Plato, your natural ruler, the philosopher-king who knows how to rule. If you want me, you must come to me, and if you insist, I may become your ruler. But I shall not come begging to you.

Did he believe that they would come? Like many great works of literature, the *Republic* shows traces that its author experienced exhilarating and extravagant hopes of success, alternating with periods of despair. Sometimes, at least, Plato hoped that they would come; that the success of his work, the fame of his wisdom, would bring them along. Then again, he felt that they would only be incited to furious attacks; that all he would bring upon himself was "an uproar of laughter and defamation"—perhaps even death.

Was he ambitious? He was reaching for the stars—for god-likeness. I sometimes wonder whether part of the enthusiasm for Plato is not due to the fact that he gave expression to many secret dreams. Even where he argues against ambition, we cannot but feel that he is inspired by it. The philosopher, he assures us, is not ambitious; although "destined to rule, he is the least eager for it." But the reason given is—that his status is too high. He who has had communion with the divine may descend from his heights to the mortals below, sacrificing himself for the sake of the interest of the state. He is not eager; but as a natural ruler and savior, he is ready to come. The poor mortals need him. Without him the state must perish, for he alone knows the secret of how to preserve it—the secret of arresting degeneration. . . .

I think we must face the fact that behind the sovereignty of the philosopher-king stands the quest for power. The beautiful portrait of the sovereign is a self-portrait. When we have recovered from the shock of this finding, we may look anew at the awe-inspiring portrait; and if we can fortify ourselves with a small dose of Socrates' irony then we may cease to find it so terrifying. We may begin to discern its human, indeed, its only too human features. We may even begin to feel a little sorry for Plato, who had to be satisfied with establishing the first professorship, instead of the first kingship, of philosophy; who could never realize his dream, the kingly Idea which he had formed after his own image. Fortified by our dose of irony, we may even find, in Plato's story, a melancholy resemblance to that innocent and unconscious little satire on Platonism, the story of the *Ugly Dachshund*, of Tono, the Great Dane, who forms his kingly Idea of "Great Dog" after his own image (but who happily finds in the end that he is Great Dog himself).

What a monument of human smallness is this idea of the philosopher-king. What a contrast between it and the simplicity and humaneness of Socrates, who warned the statesman against the danger of being dazzled by his own power, excellence, and wisdom, and who tried to teach him what matters most—that we are all frail human beings. What a decline from this world of irony and reason and truthfulness down to Plato's kingdom of the sage whose magical powers raise him high above ordinary men; although not quite high enough to forgo the use of lies, or to neglect the sorry trade of every shaman —the selling of taboos, of breeding taboos, in exchange for power over his fellow-men.

II ANCESTOR
OF DEMOCRACY

PLATO AS AN ENEMY OF DEMOCRACY:
A REJOINDER   John Wild

The most serious charge against Plato from a modern point of view is that he is an enemy of democracy. This term is now used in many ambiguous ways to cover a wide variety of meanings. Hence, the refutation of such a charge is difficult, involving as it must, an analysis of the meaning of the term *democracy* as now employed. Those who accuse Plato of being antidemocratic seldom present such an analysis. They begin by referring to passages in which Plato criticizes certain political phenomena of late fifth- and early fourth-century Athens under the name democracy. They then usually infer that Plato was an enemy of his own home city, the Athenian Democracy, as we call it, and finally conclude that he is a universal enemy of all democracy, including the great democratic ideal of modern times. Let us now examine these charges. Is it reasonable to believe that Plato was an enemy of his own home city? Is his political philosophy opposed to the modern ideal of democracy?

Plato and the Athenian Democracy

That Plato was opposed to early Greek democracy, especially as he experienced it at Athens in the last years of the great war, and

John Wild *is Professor of Philosophy, Northwestern University.* "Plato as an Enemy of Democracy: A Rejoinder" *is an excerpt from his* Plato's Modern Enemies and the Theory of Natural Law (*Chicago: The University of Chicago Press, 1953*). *Copyright 1953 by The University of Chicago. Reprinted by permission of The University of Chicago Press.*

even as it had manifested itself earlier in the Age of Pericles, must be granted. According to Plato, the ruthless imperialism of Athenian war policy and the cultural decay which followed the war must be traced back to certain sophistic movements which began in the age of Pericles. He identified this form of democracy with irresponsible anarchy and condemned it both in itself and in being the mother of tyranny. Indeed, in Book VIII of the *Republic*, he places the pure form of democracy under oligarchy and holds that it is exceeded in degeneracy only by tyranny. From this, it has been inferred that Plato must have held that democratic Athens was inferior to timocratic or oligarchic Sparta, and that he must have belonged to that minority of his fellow citizens who secretly supported Sparta.[1]

This inference, however, is very dubious, for in Book VIII of the *Republic* he is not considering concrete history, but pure social forms or abstract structures, which are never exemplified in the concrete without admixture. There is good reason to believe that Plato did not hold Athens to be a pure form of democracy, exemplifying all the corruptions described in Book VIII,[2] though it may have closely approximated this at the end of the war when he himself may have heard drunken rhetoricians clothed in armor stepping up to the rostrum to persuade the popular assembly by impassioned oratory to embark on acts of mad and hopeless aggression. He probably held that during much of its history Athens was a mixture of democracy with oligarchy and timocracy. In his view, Sparta was also not a pure timocracy, but a timocracy probably tinged with oligarchy and even tyranny. No safe conclusions concerning Plato's attitude toward his mother city can be drawn from the formalistic discussions of Book VIII of the *Republic*.

For further light on this question, we must turn to such indirect evidence as is afforded by the dialogues and to the *Epistles*, though their authenticity is dubious. An examination of all this evidence gives us good reason for holding that Plato, in spite of his bitter disapproval of many phases of Athenian policy, especially toward the end of the war, nevertheless held his own city in high filial esteem and never

[1] This common charge is made by Fite, Crossman, Popper, Toynbee, Winspear, and others.

[2] Cf. *Menexenus* 238 C-D.

took sides with Sparta or with oligarchic Athenians against his own city, as Winspear and Popper suggest.[3]

First of all, we must attach some weight to the portrait of Socrates as a loyal Athenian citizen who fought throughout the course of the war. In the light of the filial feeling he expresses toward his mother city in the *Apology* and in the *Crito*, it is inconceivable to think of him engaging in anti-Athenian activities or attitudes, though he was, no doubt, severely critical of many Athenian policies. If this is a true account, and if it is also true that Socrates was the determining influence over his whole life, it is not reasonable to believe that Plato was anti-Athenian as well as antidemocratic. If this picture is wholly or partly Plato's own creation, then Popper's supposition is even less likely. In the *Apology* Athens is referred to as "the great and mighty and wise city." [4] It is hard to think of these words as being penned by a militant enemy.

Finally, there is the first part of the Seventh *Epistle* which, if genuine, provides us with the strongest evidence of all. Here plotting for the overthrow of one's own native city is compared to patricide, and the earlier democracy is referred to as a Golden Age in comparison with the rule of the Thirty Tyrants in which Plato's uncles participated.[5] There is not a shred of evidence to support the opposed view of Popper that Plato sympathized with these oligarchic plots.

He certainly held that the skeptical, materialistic views of the sophists and rhetoricians of the Periclean Age, whom Popper calls "the Great Generation," sowed the seeds of Athenian degeneration. He was bitterly opposed to the ruthless imperialism and militarism of later Athenian policy. But this does not show that he was pro-Spartan. From his point of view, all existing states and parties were degenerate. Hence, as he states in the Seventh *Epistle*,[6] after watching the giddy course of events until his head was in a whirl, he finally decided to abandon his proposed political career and to devote his life to the study and teaching of philosophy. How can justice ever

[3] Winspear, *The Genesis of Plato's Thought*, pp. 168-70, and Popper, *The Open Society and Its Enemies*, pp. 189 ff.
[4] *Apol.* 29 D. Cf. *Crito* 51.
[5] *Epistle* VII 324 D-E.
[6] *Epistle* VII 326 ff.

be achieved until men spend some time in disciplined thought about it, and about those other basic structures which are presupposed by it?

There is no reason to distrust this assertion, which is closely approximated by many passages from the dialogues. Plato thought of his purpose as quite distinct from the policy of any existing power or party. His aim was to bring about a new cultural revolution by peaceful means—a revolution far more radical than any change which could be achieved by the shedding of blood or the mere interchange of power, a revolution of the whole human soul turning from the confused experience of the senses to an intelligible structure seen only by the eye of the mind, which might eventually culminate in the establishment of a society ruled by reason and philosophy.[7] Such a revolution has not yet been achieved. But through the ages of Western history, the influence of Plato's writings has worked in this direction.

In order to understand more clearly what Plato is criticizing under the term *democracy*, the modern reader should follow Thucydides' account of the last years of the great Peloponnesian War. Some modern interpreters have inferred from this criticism that Plato must have been a Spartan sympathizer and an enemy of his own city. Thus, according to Fite, "Plato deliberately turned his back upon the civilization of Athens—upon what is still today regarded as the highest point in Greek civilization—and embraced the barbarism of Sparta." [8] This view is shared by many other critics, including Winspear and Popper.[9] We have suggested reasons for believing that it is most hazardous.

Plato and the modern democratic ideal

Crossman,[10] Popper,[11] and others have inferred that Plato is also an enemy of *modern* democracy, filled with a bitter "hatred"

[7] Cf. *Rep.* 518 B-D.

[8] Fite, *The Platonic Legend*, p. 152.

[9] Cf. Winspear, *The Genesis of Plato's Thought*, chaps. 10, 11, especially pp. 164, 223, 225, and Popper, *op. cit.*, pp. 189 ff. Winspear and Popper, however, differ radically on Socrates. For Winspear he was, like Plato, a reactionary enemy of democracy (cf. Winspear, *Who Was Socrates?*), while for Popper he was a friend of the Periclean democracy and one of the great individualists of all times.

[10] Cf. Crossman, *Plato Today*, pp. 291 ff.

[11] Cf. Popper, *op. cit.*, chap. 10.

of democracy in general.[12] This, of course, brings up the whole question of what is now meant by "democracy." We shall not try to discuss this very complex question thoroughly. But we shall offer some reasons for holding that this inference is even more hazardous than the first one. Let us first briefly consider the chief characteristics which enter into the modern ideal of democracy and then, second, the major criticisms of Plato's *Republic* urged by certain "defenders" of this ideal.

The word *ideal* is important, for we must remember that the *Republic* is not the description of any concrete situation but the outline of a goal or standard, formulated for the guidance of action. Hence, the question we are raising should not concern the relation between this ideal and current practice, but rather its relation to the current democratic ideal. Many factors—including pre-Cartesian, realistic philosophy, Judaeo-Christian religious tradition, and skeptical elements from modern philosophy—have entered into various formulations of this ideal, which are often marked by differences in emphasis and content. In spite of these differences, it can be suggested, without arguing the historical points involved in detail, that there are at least three essential elements in the democratic ideal, each derived from one of the major movements mentioned above.

First of all, still unfinished modern struggles against feudalism and class tyranny, and the skeptical intellectual movements associated with these struggles, have contributed a deep distrust of unchecked political power and dogmatism of any kind. From this negative factor has been derived the abolition of hereditary political tenure, the right to remove public officials from office by free ballot—which is characteristic of all present-day democracies—and the separation of powers in the Constitution of the United States. This is an essential aspect of the modern democratic ideal. But when emphasized exclusively, as it often is by such modern apologists as Popper, it becomes one-sidedly negativistic, and omits other positive factors which are also essential to the democratic ideal.

When thus defended, democracy is represented as a wholly negative doctrine, its aim being exhausted in the avoidance of tyranny. All common action and government are viewed as evil, though perhaps necessary in minimal degrees. From this point of view, cooperative

[12] *Ibid.*, p. 534, *et passim.*

action of any sort is regarded as undemocratic, and the function of government is reduced to that of removing all checks to individual action, no matter how capricious or even vicious this may be. Presented in this negativistic manner, democracy would seem hard to distinguish from anarchy; and modern experience, to say nothing of the experience of the ages, has shown that freedom, when thus identified with license, leads inevitably to the domination of those who are most greedy and self-assertive, as Plato pointed out. But fortunately there are other positive factors in the democratic tradition.

From the Judaeo-Christian tradition, though not exclusively from this, it has derived a sense of the dignity and worth of human life (as opposed to oriental pessimism), the fundamental equality of all under God, and the universal brotherhood of men. These three elements, when working together, are responsible for that daring faith in the common man and that burning hope for a positive, cooperative conquest over the problems of life, which has been responsible for the recurrent dynamism of Western civilization as contrasted with the relative quietism of the East. This positive factor of faith in the common man and in his ability to cooperate in the realization of common dynamic purposes, often seemingly impossible, has made essential contributions to the still unfinished movement to abolish every trace of slavery, to other humanitarian projects, and especially to the principle of majority rule, that faith in the opinion of a majority as the wisest way of settling basic matters of common policy.

When emphasized, as it has been by certain apologists, as the very essence of democracy,[13] it is subject to certain unanswerable criticisms which have often seriously weakened the case for so-called democracy. What if the majority betrays this trust? What if, as has often happened in recent times, the majority loses all interest in freedom and democracy, and develops an urge for the easier way of tyranny? If democracy is defined exclusively in terms of majority assent, no matter what is assented to, then mass tyranny, the most awful kind, must be regarded as essentially democratic. But this is an impossible conclusion.

So fatal is this objection that Christian influences, as in the time of

[13] Cf. Locke, who defines democracy in terms of majority rule. J. Locke, *A Second Treatise on Civil Government* (New York: Van Nostrand, 1947), chap. 10, "The Forms of a Commonwealth," pp. 141-42.

Luther, making use of the religious doctrine of original sin, have often gone to the other extreme—undiluted mistrust of the common man —and have thrown their support to reactionary forms of rule. But these have been special perversions of the central stream of Christian doctrine. If man is totally depraved, the Incarnation, the central dogma of Christianity, would be absurd and impossible. Man's nature has been thwarted and damaged by sin, but it is still a genuinely human nature, made in the image of God, and retaining its immaterial faculties of reason and free choice. Hence, the appeal to reason can be made, and with divine assistance an authentic human life can still be lived in the world.

In spite of many corrupt manifestations, the Western religious influence has been felt throughout our history as predominantly hopeful and dynamic, an ever-present pressure toward the theological virtues of faith in the powers of man, a burning hope for human causes —though often seemingly hopeless—and an openness for sacrificial love. These religious factors have an essential place in the modern democratic ideal. But to be purified of dangerous fantasy and delusion, they need to be reinforced by a third influence.

This is derived from the tradition of realistic philosophy which originated in ancient Greece, and has since been cultivated and refined and developed down to the present day. It was this tradition that first worked out a clear and articulate theory of natural law, natural rights, and natural duties which has played a decisive, positive role in the evolution of democratic concepts and practices. In the Middle Ages it was merged with Christian faith, often in such a way as to be almost overwhelmed by it. Hence, many modern writers have failed to focus it as a distinct doctrine having an integrity of its own, and have viewed it as a mere appendage to religious dogma. As a matter of fact, however, as we shall see, it was independently developed by Plato and Aristotle, apart from any Christian influence.

This tradition has contributed to the democratic tradition a definition of human goodness as the realization of a nature shared by all men. It has also defined certain universal rights and duties prescribed by such realization, which are binding on all men and on all communities. Such principles are permanent and inalienable by any form of tyranny. They are prescribed not by any ruler, class, or arbitrary constitution, but by nature itself and the cosmic powers which produce man. They remain in force no matter what a human majority may decide, and must be clearly recognized by any rationally ordered society in which authentic human life is to be possible. Hence, modern democratic communities offer protection to the weak and evanescent human individual, who alone possesses the precious faculty of reason, against ruling opinion. No matter what a majority may decide, these principles remain in force; the ruling opinion may be in error. Free discussion and criticism must proceed. Hence, in all genuinely democratic countries the rights of access to information, of assembly, and of free expression of opinion are recognized and protected.

The United Nations Declaration of Human Rights specifies *other* rights presupposed by these, such as the right to sufficient nurture and medical care and the right to education. In Great Britain and the United States education is not yet recognized as a *right*, but there is a general understanding that adequate training of the cognitive powers is required for the intelligent exercise of democratic functions, which has already led to the establishment of public schools and universities. This recognition of the importance of reason as the only power naturally fitted for the guidance of human life, and of those individual rights which are required for its exercise, is the peculiar contribution of realistic philosophy to the modern ideal of democracy.

When exclusively emphasized, as in ancient times by Plato and Aristotle, this natural-law tradition has produced political ideals which stress the rule of reason—the realization of basic human needs, especially the need for rational nurture and education. Compared with the least inadequate statements of the modern democratic ideal, such as the United Nations Declaration of Human Rights, the more extreme formulations of the natural-law ideal, like Plato's *Republic*, suffer from a lack of certain elements provided by the other two sources we have noted. We miss some of the effective checks against dogmatism and tyranny which have been discovered in modern times, and a robust faith in the capacities of the common man for practical insight and sacrificial endeavor. But in the *Republic* at least we find that these are not wholly lacking.

Plato also was acutely aware of the dangers of tyranny. As a protection against it, he suggested a concentration of community energy on the primary task of education, and a system of rigorous civil service examinations for public office. That other protections are advisable may be granted. But that this must always be the most basic protection is, at least, an arguable point. Plato may have had an exaggerated conception of hereditary differences in intellectual endowment. But he certainly recognized the *basic* unity of all men as possessing a common human nature and the need for giving equal opportunity to all. His *Republic* is not a hereditary caste society. The theory of natural law, which lies at the heart of his whole conception, is still an essential ingredient in our modern democratic ideal.

In view of these facts, it is reasonable to hold that Plato's *Republic*, when compared with the modern ideal of democracy, is deficient in certain respects, but not totally opposed to this ideal or essentially undemocratic, as is often supposed. This ideal, one-sided as it may be, is not so deficient as those antirational interpretations of democracy which identify it with philosophical skepticism and anarchy or with unrestrained majority rule. We shall now attempt to confirm these tentative conclusions by a brief consideration of the major objections which are urged against Plato by modern "democratic" apologists.

Class rule

Many commentators repeat the charge that Plato in the *Republic* is defending an aristocracy in the sense of a small privileged class or caste, ruling for its own interests. Thus, according to Fite,[14] the whole community is an "aristocratic Republic" to be controlled by "a ruling-class," [15] a privileged minority. He claims that this is the Spartan ideal of a regimented state.[16] These charges are repeated by Crossman,[17] Winspear, and Popper.[18] The most extreme version of this criticism is in Popper's "elite," [20] a "ruling class," [21] a "master

[14] Fite, *op. cit.*, chap. 7.

[15] *Ibid.*, pp. 134 ff. Cf. Vlastos, "Slavery in Plato's Thought," *Philosophical Review*, L (1941), 291-92. Hoernle refers to Plato's guardians as "a governing class" and "a selected élite." Hoernle, "Would Plato Have Approved of the National Socialist State?" *Philosophy*, XIII (1938), 172.

[16] *Ibid.*, p. 152.

[17] Crossman, *op. cit.*, pp. 265 ff.

[18] Winspear, *The Genesis of Plato's Thought*, chap. 11.

[19] Popper, *op. cit.*, p. 134.

[20] *Ibid.*, p. 40.

[21] *Ibid.*, p. 50.

race," [22] and "herders of human cattle," [23] are a hereditary caste selected on racial grounds.[24] Beginning with this last of Popper's
charges, it is quite clear that Plato's guardians (φύλακες) are in no
sense arbitrary rulers, but guardians of a law of nature, which they
have in no sense decreed or determined but have discovered by rational dialectic. Popper's slanted translations, for which he offers no
justification, are perhaps to be explained as a result of his legal positivism, which regards any law whatsoever as the expression of an
arbitrary and tyrannical preference. It is only from such a standpoint
that these translations become understandable.

But it is hard to see how, then, rational government can be distinguished from tyranny. If there are no basic practical principles
which can be recognized by reason, then all government is the expression of arbitrary preference and, therefore, equally tyrannical.[25] Yet
Popper himself certainly opposes "the open society" to what he calls
dictatorship and tyranny. What, then, is this open society? Either it
is a community with no government or the very minimum of cooperative action, in which case he is defending a diluted anarchism; or it is
merely a form of unjustifiable, arbitrary rule to which everyone agrees,
in which case he is defending mass tyranny. With respect to these
alternatives, we may certainly ask the moral relativist for evidence to
show either that anarchy is possible for man or that mass tyranny,
in the light of recent political experience, is not the most dangerous
form of oppression.

Moral relativism, of course, is not Plato's point of view. He believed
that all men possess a partly rational nature in common, and that
this nature includes basic tendencies which must be cooperatively
realized if human life is to be lived.[26] To understand these essential
tendencies is to grasp the moral law. Plato's guardians are not arbitrary rulers at all, but guardians of the law, who try first to understand it, then to apply it for the benefit of the whole community,
including themselves, and finally to preserve it through the flux of

[22] *Ibid.*, p. 146.
[23] *Ibid.*, p. 52.
[24] *Ibid.*, pp. 50 ff., 148 ff. Crossman makes the same charge. Cf. Crossman,
op. cit., p. 132.
[25] Hoernle's comparison of the *Republic* with the national socialist state is based
on a relativism of this kind. Cf. Hoernle, *op. cit.*, p. 168-69.
[26] Cf. *Rep.* 369 B 5-6.

varying circumstance. They are not a hereditary caste. At *Republic* 415 C 3 and at 423 C 8 he clearly states that all citizens are eligible to become guardians, including the children of artisans, whom Popper calls "drudges," and female children. Plato has a rather extreme view of the importance of heredity in these matters; so he believes that guardians will tend to produce guardians. But he specifically provides for exceptions. No child of a guardian will be chosen for office simply on the grounds of birth. He must show his special qualifications by meeting very stringent tests and examinations which are given to all. This is not a caste society.

Nor is it correctly described as "class rule" in the usual sense of this word—government by a privileged group for the attainment of special interests denied to others. Plato's guardians and auxiliaries are not a *class* in this sense. They are civil servants selected by rigorous examinations for the performance of certain functions necessary to the attainment of the common good. The development of a sense of *class* distinctions and *class* interests is the sign of social decline. In the *Republic* all are friends and mutual supporters of one another.[27] Popper speaks constantly of the "privileges" of the guardians. But in Plato's view the sound exercise of the governing function for the common good is no privilege, but a burdensome responsibility. If the guardians do anything for their own special interests, they are obstructing the common good and thus betraying their function. They are provided with no material goods beyond their necessary needs, and live an arduous life, intensively devoted to a common good in which, of course, they justly share. Even though we may disagree with such a view, it is not correct to refer to it as the rule of a privileged class in the modern sense of this word.

Plato is often attacked as a defender of slavery. According to Popper, all the inhabitants of the *Republic* except the guardians are in a state of slavery.[28] If by *slave* we mean a human being whose natural rights are disregarded and violated, this charge is certainly erroneous. The artisans perform productive functions for which they are naturally fitted. As rational beings, they are given the same edu-

---

[27] The guardians are referred to as: "Friends and supporters of whose freedom they had been the guardians," *Rep.* 547 C 1; "saviors and helpers," *Rep.* 463 B 1-2.

[28] Popper, *op. cit.*, chap. 6. Vlastos, *op. cit.*, p. 293, and Farrington, *Greek Science*, Penguin ed., I, 142, both preceded Popper in making this charge.

cation primarily in music and gymnastics that is given to all, until they reach the age of twenty.[29] If Plato had been able to conceive of modern machine production, he might have extended this age and modified his whole scheme. But unfortunately this lay beyond the range of his imagination. Necessary material artifacts must be produced by the labor of the artisans. But they are allowed to have adequate property to satisfy their material needs, though an upper limit is set.[30] Their material standard of living is higher than that of the guardians; their fundamental rights are recognized; they participate in all the fruits of communal endeavor. They are not slaves, unless an unusual meaning is given to this word.

The question as to whether Plato takes slaves for granted in the *Republic*, but never refers to them, is a controversial one. I believe that the answer is definitely *no* in view of his explicit remarks at *Republic* 547 C ff. where the introduction of slavery is attributed to the class feeling and violence which attends the establishment of a timocratic state. The timocratic "aristocrats" "enslave their own people who formerly (in the ideal *Republic*) lived as free men under their guardianship . . . and holding them as slaves and drudges, devote themselves to war (as in Sparta) and to keeping these subjects in bondage." To this we may also add the further argument that slaves in the *Republic* would be superfluous, since all the necessary productive functions are performed by artisans whose natural rights, including the right to an education, are definitely recognized. If this is true, Plato's imagination was politically far ahead of his own time, as it certainly was in the case of the rights of women.

Lying propaganda

As a result of our intellectual heritage, of which Plato and Platonism are important parts, we have attained a respect for reason and truth, and a deep sense of the need for an educated and informed

---

[29] Otherwise, the selection of prospective guardians specifically referred to at *Rep.* 415 C 3 and 423 C 8 would be impossible. The early literary education (music and gymnastics) which continues to the age of twenty (*Rep.* 537 B) will also include mathematics and science, though taught in a "playful manner" quite distinct from the serious study of these subjects by the prospective guardians between the ages of 20 and 30. Cf. *Rep.* 536 E ff.

[30] *Rep.* 422.

electorate, if democracy is to be maintained. Hence, the idea of rulers who deceive the people rightly offends us as undemocratic. Plato's defense of the "noble lie" at *Republic* 414 B strikes us as peculiarly obnoxious and even reminds us of unscrupulous totalitarian propaganda. This objection has been singled out for special emphasis by political thinkers like Crossman and Popper. Thus, Crossman interprets the passage as an approval of noble lies for "cajoling the civilian masses into obedience." [31]

Popper's accusations are even more violent. He compares this procedure to the activities of the nefarious Nazi Propaganda Bureau, and attacks the noble lie of Plato as an attempt to infuse racialist doctrines of blood and soil and the master race into the innocent inhabitants of the republic.[32] I am not prepared to defend Plato's concept of the noble lie in all respects; but I believe that these charges rest on serious misunderstandings.

First of all, Plato has a somewhat elaborate and complex doctrine concerning the lie,[33] which may be summarized as follows: the worst kind of lie, according to him, is "the lie in the soul," the belief by one's self of what is not so, whether or not the truth is suspected. Such lying to one's self is involuntary, for no one really wishes to be deceived. Hence, it is utterly indefensible, unmitigatedly evil without exception. Socratic education—radical questioning of self—is required to root it out. What *we* commonly refer to as *a lie* is something quite distinct. This consists in telling someone else what the teller himself knows to be false, because he knows what is really true. In Plato's view, this is secondary and derivative, for at least someone knows the truth. Hence, he calls this merely a lie in words. Such a liar is not deceiving himself, unless he is using the lie for a mistaken or immoral purpose. If so, it involves a lie in his soul, which is a disastrous evil. Sometimes, however, the lie in words is justifiable. This is when those to whom we are communicating are not in a position to understand or gain any benefit from the truth which we understand.

Thus, at the beginning of the *Republic*,[34] Socrates brings up the

[31] Crossman, *op. cit.*, p. 275.
[32] Popper, *op. cit.*, pp. 136-41.
[33] *Rep.* 382 A-C. Cf. 535 E.
[34] *Rep.* 331 C.

case of someone who has lent us a deadly weapon and suddenly returns to demand it from us in a fit of homicidal mania. In such a case, it would seem reasonable for us to say that we had left it somewhere else or misplaced it. Another less extreme case is that of children who may ask us questions, the abstract answers to which they are not as yet able to understand. When they ask, we usually give them some concrete story or picture, which may convey something of the truth to them, but certainly not the clear, abstract truth as we understand it. We do not refer to such practices as lying. Plato, whose standards in this respect are very high, calls this "a lie in words." He says that the guardians of the ideal republic are in a similar situation. They possess a coherent body of abstract knowledge concerning human nature and the obscure noetic powers of man—the source of human unity—which they cannot explain in full detail to the artisans and auxiliaries, who see radically different functions being performed by different members of the community.

No society can live in a healthy state unless there is an underlying sense of unity and a feeling of devotion to the common purpose. The full nature of this purpose and the complex doctrine on which it is based cannot be fully explained. So the guardians simplify it and clothe it in the concrete imagery of a patriotic myth of common origin and of different natural endowment fitting men for different functions in the cooperative living of human life. This is the "noble lie"—a simplified version of the truth concerning diversified endowments and common origin, like simplified heroic versions of past history, and other symbols capable of eliciting group loyalty and common aspiration.

I believe that Plato over-emphasized the need for such patriotic mythologies, but it is at least true that all human communities so far have developed them. In any case, this is the noble lie. The guardians know that it is not exactly true. Nevertheless, in a simplified version it does convey the gist of the truth. Men are brothers, though the earth is not their common mother. Souls are not gold or silver; this is mythological language. But that some are endowed with superior intelligence is true. The purpose of the myth is to elicit feelings of brotherhood and loyalty to the whole community as members of one family. This purpose is morally sound, though not exactly and abstractly stated. So this is a lie in words, a noble lie.

Popper claims that this myth is an expression of racialism.[35] "These metals are hereditary, they are racial characteristics." [36] This is a *non sequitur*. We may grant that the metals refer to what Plato held to be hereditary tendencies toward greater or less intelligence. But from this it does not follow that these differences are racial. Racial traits are hereditary, but all hereditary traits are not racial.

According to Popper, the purpose of the myth is to emphasize these differences, and to strengthen "the rule of the master race." [37] As a matter of fact, Plato makes it quite clear that the purpose is rather that of emphasizing a unity of race, so far as race means common ancestry, and thus of eliciting a loyalty to the whole community which transcends differences of intelligence and social function.[38]

If, as Popper supposes, the guardians were using this myth as political propaganda to support their own unjust rule, they would be guilty, on Plato's view, of ignorance and self-deception concerning the most important matters—the lie in the soul.

Thought control

Philosophical skeptics, like Crossman and Popper, for whom the very concept of philosophical truth is synonymous with dogmatism, accuse Plato of advocating a tyrannical form of thought control, which strikes at the very heart of democracy. Thus, Crossman says that the greatest flaw in the reasoning of the *Republic* is that "human reason is capable of infallibility and that the scientific spirit should be prepared to force others to accept it as infallible." [39] Popper asserts that the *Republic* rests on "an educational monopoly of the ruling class with the strictest censorship, even of oral debates," and opposes this to the intellectualism of Socrates which "was fundamentally equalitarian and individualistic." [40] This criticism raises a certain question of fact, as well as the basic issue of philosophic truth which underlies the whole debate.

That Plato was intensely critical of the dominant art of his own

[35] Popper, *op. cit.*, pp. 138 ff. Cf. pp. 553-55.
[36] *Ibid.*, p. 138.
[37] *Ibid.*
[38] *Rep.* 415 D 3. Cf. 414 E 2, 415 A 3 and A 8.
[39] Crossman, *op. cit.*, p. 277.
[40] Popper, *op. cit.*, p. 130.

time, including that of Homer, on philosophical grounds, and that he defended a policy of censorship with respect to art which might exercise a demoralizing influence on the young, must be granted. I believe that he went too far in this direction, and that censorship beyond the period of youth should be left to the educated individual to exercise for himself. But is it true that the citizens of the *Republic* are to be passively molded and indoctrinated with one theory alone— "oral debates" being eliminated—so that they are to be totally unfamiliar with any opposed point of view? This would, indeed, be a vicious blow at intellectual freedom, the very heart of true democracy. Both Crossman and Popper assert that this is the case. But in the *Republic* itself there is no evidence to support this view.

The work is a dialogue in which Thrasymachus, Glaucon, Adeimantus are given ample opportunity to express opposed views. Surely, we make take this as an indication of what Plato would regard as a normal mode of argument in his ideal community. For him, Socrates remained the ideal teacher, and the dialectical method of question and answer, in which the mind is free to take any position whatsoever and to follow the argument wherever it may lead, remained the ideal form of intellectual procedure. Even the soul, when thinking within herself, follows this dialectical pattern.[41] There is no statement in the *Republic* which provides any legitimate basis for the thesis that the expression of certain opinions is to be suppressed. Of course, many opinions are not to be accepted. But this is because they are constantly shown to be unable to meet the Socratic test of maintaining themselves in searching questioning and debate. There is no suggestion that the nonguardians of the republic, when they reach maturity, are to be kept in a state of artificial ignorance concerning such false doctrines. In fact, there is definite evidence pointing clearly in the opposite direction.

At every stage of education after the elementary level, the students are to be given examinations to test their advance. Some of these tests are to be moral, but others are intellectual.[42] The students are to be presented with false doctrines of every kind, defended with the greatest possible skill in order to test their capacity to see through

[41] *Theaet.* 189 E 4 ff.
[42] *Rep.* III 412 D 7 ff.

fallacies and to avoid becoming confused by clever argument.[43] Any opinion can be expressed by anyone. There is no restraint on freedom of thought. Without such freedom the whole concept of Platonic argument and education would be absurd. But not every opinion can be accepted as true.

The *Republic* is an imagined ideal community which in Plato's conception demands the discovery of actual truths, especially concerning the most important and basic matters of a moral and philosophic nature. Crossman and Popper claim that there are no such truths.[44] Therefore, they cannot distinguish between the claim to possess such truth and undiluted dogmatism and tyranny. As we have already suggested, this is the basic philosophical issue between Plato and his most bitter critics. This is why they attempt to defend a violent contrast between Socrates, "the agnostic," who believed in no "final truth" at all and Plato, the totalitarian dogmatist, who betrayed his master by openly defending an articulate and full-fledged philosophy.[45]

We have already called attention to the dubious nature of the thesis that Socrates himself was a pure agnostic in the light of the *Apology*, which Popper accepts as genuinely Socratic.[46] At this point, we shall add only a brief comment on the *Gorgias*, which he also holds to be a true picture of Socrates.[47] In this dialogue Socrates presents a long and elaborate defense of the distinction between true and false art, and the relation of the arts to one another,[48] argues at length in defense of his positive belief that doing injustice is worse than suffering it,[49] analyzes the virtues as they are analyzed in Book IV of the *Republic*,[50] clearly defends the distinction between human goodness and pleasure,[51] and expresses a definite belief in immortality

[43] *Rep.* 413 B 1-3.
[44] Cf. Crossman, *op. cit.*, pp. 275 ff., and Popper, *op. cit.*, chap. 5. Cf. note 11, p. 580.
[45] Crossman, *op. cit.*, chaps. 3-4, and Popper, *op. cit.*, pp. 130-31, 184-95.
[46] Popper, *op. cit.*, pp. 598-603.
[47] *Ibid.*, pp. 593, 603.
[48] *Gorg.* 463 ff.
[49] *Gorg.* 467-80.
[50] *Rep.* 506 C ff.
[51] *Gorg.* 495-503.

and a detailed, mythical picture of the fate of the soul in the after-life.[52] Is this agnosticism?

Socrates was certainly an enemy of uncriticized opinion and preju-dice. He believed that all ideas must be subjected to the test of free argument and debate, as Plato also believed. But where in any dia-logue, in Xenophon, or anywhere else, is there any evidence to sup-port the view that Socrates held all truth to be unobtainable? If this negativistic doctrine is true, how can we, then, avoid the conclusion that Socrates' passionate quest for philosophic truth, to which he devoted his life, was a stupid mistake? What is the use of going on seeking for something that cannot in any sense be found? Of course, even the theory that there is no philosophic truth, if true, is a philo-sophic truth, requiring justification and support. Even this is a philosophy. Was it the philosophy of Socrates? If it was, we cannot trust the *Apology*, the *Gorgias*, or any dialogue of Plato or Xenophon —or indeed any evidence available to us. What, then, shall we trust?

Plato, who knew the man, did not accept this negativistic theory. He certainly held that Socrates' quest was not futile—that he had found certain truths, at least those suggested in the *Apology*, that there is something higher than man, that man is more than a mass of flesh and bones, that the cultivation of the soul is more important than the cultivation of the body, that vice is worse than death, etc. In his own life he attempted to elaborate the implications of these Socratic convictions. In doing this, he did not merely repeat what Socrates himself had said; he went further. Was this a betrayal? If so, the whole history of Western thought in its major currents has been a betrayal of Socrates. Can the modern ideal of democracy be defended and justified against other alternatives on the basis of a complete philosophical skepticism? Can freedom of thought be ade-quately maintained without some true insight into the nature of freedom, the nature of thought, and the complex nature of man? If so, democracy will be preserved by accident or historic destiny rather than by responsible human choice and effort.

[52] *Gorg.* 523 to end.

The attack on Plato: conclusion

We have now studied the major criticisms urged against Plato by his modern enemies: first, that he is a dogmatist; second, a Spartan militarist and advocate of ruthless force and violence; third, a totalitarian defender of historicism; fourth, a racialist; fifth, an enemy of individual freedom, working for the return of a tribal, closed society; and finally, sixth, a militant opponent not only of ancient democracy but of modern democracy as well. Having examined these charges in the light of evidence provided by the dialogues, our conclusions may be summarized as follows:

1. Plato is a dogmatist only in the sense in which anyone defending basic philosophical convictions is a dogmatist. In this sense, Socrates was also a dogmatist, for even if the *Apology* alone is accepted as an authentic picture of him, he held many basic philosophical convictions. Uncriticized opinion and prejudice are inimical to freedom. But unless freedom is identified with anarchy, it has nothing to fear either from critical knowledge, which is able to defend itself by reference to evidence available to all, or from the untrammeled search for such knowledge in every field of human experience.

2. Plato's impatience with social corruption and his zeal for reform may have led him at times to make statements which seem to imply an approval of militant means to achieve what he conceived to be worthy ends. Such statements cannot be defended when separated from their contexts. The facts known about Plato's life, however, and what can be reasonably inferred from his writings in general give no ground for attributing to him any sympathy for militaristic and dictatorial practices or attitudes. So far as his definite doctrines are concerned, they are antimilitaristic and uncompromisingly attack all aggressive use of force. In this respect, Plato's social philosophy is very close to that of Toynbee, in spite of Toynbee's anti-Platonic polemic.

3. Plato is not an idealist, and the organic theory of society, as well as political totalitarianism, are altogether foreign to his thought. The human community, as he conceives it, is neither a mere juxta-

position of atomic individuals nor a superorganism living its own life apart from the individual members. It is rather a group of individuals unified by a shared purpose capable of eliciting cooperative acts—not a physical or substantial unity, but a moral unity of purpose and aspiration. Neglect of reason and rational nurture thus lead to social disintegration and attack the community at its very roots.

4. The charge of racialism seems to have no justification, for the distinction between Greek and barbarian has no implication of racial inferiority in the modern sense. A traditional cultural enemy is not necessarily a racial inferior, and was not so conceived by Plato. An interest in eugenics does not imply the theory of a master race. Plato's myths of creation are all unitarian. The whole human race is one flock under one divine shepherd. Human cultures may vary widely in their excellence, but human nature is everywhere the same.

5. The *Republic* is a universal ideal to be approximated in the concrete realm of flux, not the description of any past Golden Age. Plato was opposed to degeneration—change from a better to a worse state—but not to change in general, which he recognized as an essential trait of physical existence. The *Republic* is no more a closed society than any other rationally articulated social ideal. Even the most piecemeal social engineering must be guided by some such articulated conception of the ultimate end to be striven for. If by *tribal* is meant a society ruled by uncriticized prejudice and arbitrary decree, the *Republic* is certainly not a tribal society.

6. Plato was opposed to the hysterical mob rule which he knew by the name "democracy" and which he had experienced at first hand during the end of the great war. He was also opposed to the philosophical skepticism and relativism which it presupposes. But there is a grave question as to whether the inference that Plato must, therefore, be opposed to modern democracy is justifiable, since this is a complex idea to which many historical movements have contributed. Three movements especially have made essential contributions to this modern ideal of democracy: first, skeptical ways of thought associated with the modern rebellions against feudalism and class oppression; second, an appreciation of the dignity and worth of human existence and a trust in the common man, derived primarily from Christianity; and finally, the concept of natural law as equally bind-

ing upon all men everywhere, and a respect for reason and rational education, contributed by Greek philosophy and its later developments.

Plato's ideal is, of course, most closely related to the last. But it is not totally deficient in the other two respects. He also hated tyranny and suggested ways of guarding against it, especially Socratic education. Nor was he devoid of all sense of the worth of individual life and the natural equality of men as possessing a common human nature. Plato's ideal may reasonably be described as deficient from a democratic point of view, but not as antidemocratic, unless the democratic ideal is uncritically identified with anarchism.

Reasons for the attack: misunderstanding of Plato's moral philosophy

If these conclusions are not entirely mistaken we must regard the widespread opinion that Platonic thought is somehow deeply opposed to all modern progressive ideals as a tragic misunderstanding, and we must raise the question as to why it is that able thinkers have been seemingly so predisposed to embrace it. Why is it that these dialogues, which in the past have aroused so many minds to Socratic questioning and the impassioned quest for philosophic truth, why is it that they have recently been studied by so many English and American thinkers with so little sympathy and understanding?

One basic reason we have had occasion to comment on. This is the subjectivist trend of modern thought and the skeptical distrust of philosophic reason which have now come to exert such a dominant influence not only on academic thought but on common-sense philosophy as well. Such skepticism places a yawning chasm between the present-day reader and the unhesitant realism of Plato and Aristotle, who accepted the fact of human knowledge, and dared to apply their cognitive faculties to the most obscure and basic questions. It is so easy for us to confuse this trust in reason with naïve dogmatism, and to ignore or misconstrue the actual evidence offered in its defense.

There are no doubt other reasons connected with Plato's style. But whatever the causes may be, there is a surprising vagueness and diversity of opinion among Plato's modern critics, and even among his more careful commentators, concerning the nature of his moral doctrine.

In Germany the word *eudaemonism* is widely used in this connection. Thus, in Ueberweg's monumental *Grudriss der Philosophie* we are told that "Plato's Ethics is eudaemonistic." [53] But its present-day connotations are not the same. Having been widely used by idealistic thinkers, like Paulsen, it now suggests to the modern reader a theory of self-realization according to which the human good is regarded as a maximal satisfaction of any interests that happen to prevail in a given institution or society. Without any stable criterion for distinguishing what is essential from what is incidental and ephemeral, such a view is closely allied to utilitarianism and other forms of moral relativism.

Hence it is not surprising that in Anglo-Saxon countries where utilitarianism is very influential, Socratic and Platonic ethics are often referred to as utilitarian. Professor Fite is not niggardly in attributing diverse views to Plato, but utilitarianism is one which plays an important role in his campaign of vilification and attack. According to him, Platonic ethics lack any warmth of personal feeling. "His attitude towards truth, moral or other truth, is everywhere impersonal and objective." [54] Socrates also is a Spencerian moral mechanist attempting to settle moral issues by a quantitative calculus. Thus in commenting on the *Gorgias* he writes: "Socrates is still as ever a utilitarian only now (from the Spencerian point of view) a more scientific utilitarian. In both dialogues the ethics is an ethics of calculation." [55]

As we have already noted, the opposite view of Plato as a philosopher of rigid repression haunted by scenes of debauchery is also expressed by Fite and by others. Thus, Niebuhr conceives of Plato as a "dualistic" thinker for whom everything connected with the body is evil.[56] Winspear, for whom Plato is "an idealistic, authoritarian reactionary," [57] shares his view. According to him, "the logical (and historical) outcome of Platonic theory was asceticism, and an asce-

[53] Praechter, *Die Philosophie des Altertums* (Berlin: E. S. Mittler, 1926), I, 336.
[54] Fite, *The Platonic Legend*, p. 184.
[55] *Ibid.*, pp. 189-90.
[56] Niebuhr, *Nature and Destiny of Man*, I, 31-33.
[57] *The Genesis of Plato's Thought*, p. 228.

ticism which became increasingly stern and harsh" [58] (*The Genesis of Plato's Thought*, p. 214). Crossman also repudiates any eudaemonistic interpretation of Plato whose "bias in favor of aristocracy led him to identify the 'gentleman' with the good man. . . ." [59] But Plato was not concerned about the human welfare of even this favored class, since he demanded of them "a virtue far beyond their reach," while to the "lower orders" he denied "any possibility of self-realization." [60]

None of these commentators pays any attention to Plato's constant use of the term *nature* in a normative sense. Popper, however, does notice this, and rightly sees that the concept of *nature* plays a determining role in the whole structure of Platonic ethics.[61] He refers to this doctrine as "Spiritual naturalism." But he can see nothing determinate in the term nature. Hence "spiritual naturalism can be used to defend anything, and especially any 'positive,' i.e., existing norms." [62] He thinks that the *nature* of a thing, according to Plato, is its "origin." [63] The more ancient something is, the more natural it is. Hence this view reduces to a reactionary moral conservatism. As we have indicated, it is possible to show that this is certainly not Plato's meaning. But then what did he mean? What is the Platonic moral philosophy?

It is only by attaining a satisfactory answer to this question that we may hope to explain the misunderstandings we have been considering, and the variety of conflicting views attributed to him by his modern critics. Surely all these attributions cannot be correct. I believe it will be possible to show that none of them is. Plato's realistic ethics of natural law represents a mode of thought diverging fundamentally from the dominant subjectivist trend of modern philosophy. During the nineteenth century this tradition was completely submerged. Hence it is no wonder that modern interpreters of Plato have difficulty in focusing it.

As we have seen, almost every influential modern ethical position has been imputed to Plato. The Germans have confused him with

[58] *Ibid.*, p. 214.
[59] *Plato Today*, p. 266.
[60] *Ibid.*, pp. 266-67.
[61] *Open Society* (Eng. ed.), pp. 61 ff.
[62] *Ibid.*, pp. 61-62.
[63] *Ibid.*, p. 64.

Kant, the English with utilitarianism. Many other views have also been attributed to him. But with a few exceptions no one has recently thought of him in connection with the realistic tradition of natural law, of which he was actually a founder. These exceptions, however, deserve to be mentioned.

One is Professor Solmsen who in his recent book *Plato's Theology* has dared to question the accepted opinion that natural-law philosophy began with the Stoics.[64] The other is Mr. H. Cairns in his book on *Legal Philosophy from Plato to Hegel*, who suggests that "by insisting upon a rigid distinction between the idea of law and the positive enactments of the State, Plato prepared the way for natural-law speculation and the perception of an ideal element in law making." [65] These assertions are made incidentally and are left undeveloped by their authors. But they constitute noteworthy exceptions. For the most part, Plato's moral realism, like the concept of natural law itself, has been unnoticed and confused with essentially alien tendencies more familiar to the modern mind.

Thus in spite of their diversity, the views which the modern critics of Plato attribute to him all have one thing in common, that norms are man-made constructions, legislated into existence by arbitrary human interest or decree. It is quite clear, . . . that Plato held no such conception. As a matter of fact, he identified this sort of moral subjectivism with his enemies, the sophists, and bitterly attacked it in his dialogues. What an irony that in a time when subjectivism has become almost a philosophical truism, a peculiarly obnoxious variety of it should be imputed to Plato himself! In fact, . . . Plato was a moral realist. As such, he must be classified with the tradition which later came to be known as that of *natural law*. Unless we succeed in clearly focusing Plato's moral realism, we shall never understand the confusions we have been discussing, nor the resulting issues between him and his modern critics.

[64] *Plato's Theology* (Ithaca: Cornell University Press, 1942), pp. 167 and 184.
[65] H. Cairns, *Legal Philosophy from Plato to Hegel* (Baltimore: Johns Hopkins Press, 1949), p. 37.

PLATO AND THE MORAL FOUNDATION

OF DEMOCRACY   John H. Hallowell

There is no more vivid description of the transition from
democracy to tyranny than that contained in the eighth book of
Plato's *Republic*. Reading it today, we are impressed with its striking
relevance to the contemporary political scene, and there is no greater
tribute to the enduring wisdom of Plato than that fact. That Plato
himself was not attached to democracy as a form of government does
not lessen the relevance of his analysis. If we mean by democracy
the unrestrained rule of the many in their own interest, then this was
a form of government regarded as perverted not only by Plato and
Aristotle but by the framers of our own Constitution. The constitutional, representative democracy which the framers of our Constitution established bears considerable resemblance to that form of government which Aristotle described as a "polity" and which he regarded as the best practicable of all constitutions.

I

The transition from democracy to tyranny is described by
Plato as a process of both individual and social disintegration, and
the latter is depicted as having its roots in the former. When the
individual revolts against tradition and authority, when instinct and

John H. Hallowell *is Professor of Political Science, Duke University.*
"Plato and the Moral Foundation of Democracy" is an excerpt from
his The Moral Foundation of Democracy (*Chicago: The University*
of Chicago Press, 1954). Copyright 1954 by the University of Chi-
cago. Reprinted by permission of The University of Chicago Press.

desire are exalted above reason, when intellect is subordinated to will, when all desires become lawful and no standard is left for choosing among them, then at last a master-passion, "as leader of the soul, takes madness for the captain of its guard and breaks out in frenzy; if it can lay hold upon any thoughts or desires that are of good report and still capable of shame, it kills them or drives them forth, until it has purged the soul of all sobriety and called in the partisans of madness to fill the vacant place." [1] And just as a single tyrant desire takes possession of the individual who knows no restraints, so the mass of individuals in a society that knows no restraints at last submit their wills to the will of a tyrant, in order that they might escape the tyranny of their own passions. Freedom, now having become license, becomes an intolerable burden, and they seek to escape from it by submission to the tyrant. Erich Fromm has described this escape from freedom in modern psychological terms; but the more profound analysis was suggested by Plato five centuries before Christ. There is no more accurate description of Hitler and his kind than Plato's description of the despotic man who, like a lunatic, "dreams that he can lord it over all mankind and heaven besides." For "when nature or habit or both have combined the traits of drunkenness, lust, and lunacy, then you have the perfect specimen of the despotic man." [2]

The despotic man and the despotic state are but the end-products of a progressive degeneration that begins when ambition usurps the rule of reason. At first, ambition is motivated by a love of honor and is an ambition to serve. This honorable ambition gives way in time to the passion for wealth. From a means to life, wealth increasingly becomes the end of life. At first, the passion for wealth holds the appetitive desires in check; but to the extent that it encourages the luxurious indulgence of the body, to the extent that the many are pauperized to satisfy the insatiable cravings of the few, the appetitive desires are increasingly "liberated" from restraint, and anarchy in the soul and society is the result. The man who is "under the sway of a host of unnecessary pleasures and appetites" replaces the "miserly oligarch" as the dominant type of man in society. "His life is subject

[1] *The Republic of Plato*, trans. F. M. Cornford (London, 1945), p. 298. Quoted with permission of the Oxford University Press.
[2] *Ibid.*, p. 298.

to no order or restraint," and freedom comes to mean to do as one pleases. The parent falls into the habit of behaving like the child, the father is afraid of his sons, and children have neither fear nor respect for their parents. The teacher flatters his pupils, and the pupils repay the flattery with contempt. Family bonds are loosened, and promiscuous sexual indulgence replaces marital fidelity. "The citizens become so sensitive that they resent the slightest application of control as intolerable tyranny, and in their resolve to have no master they end by disregarding even the law, written or unwritten." [3]

Bred by the spirit of license, a class of drones emerges which takes possession of political offices, intent upon nothing more than occupying them for their own advantage. At the same time, another class is steadily bent upon the amassing of wealth. And it is this class which provides provender for the drones. A third class, the largest of all, is composed of the people with few possessions and little or no interest in politics. The plundered rich, in an effort to protect their wealth from the drones, become more and more reactionary. Eventually, in an effort to protect themselves from both the drones and the reactionary rich, the people put forward a single champion of their interests.

"In the early days he has a smile and a greeting for everyone he meets; disclaims any absolute power; makes large promises to his friends and to the public; sets about the relief of debtors and the distribution of the land to the people and to his supporters." [4] But soon the people's champion begins to act more and more like a despot. "If he suspects some of cherishing thoughts of freedom and not submitting to his rule," he finds pretexts for doing away with them. He requests a private army to protect him from the enemies of the people; but what is first looked upon as a popular militia to protect the people's interests gradually turns into a weapon with which to exploit the people and keep them in bondage. "The bolder spirits among those who have helped him to power and now hold positions of influence will begin to speak their mind of him and among themselves to criticize his policy. If the despot is to maintain his rule, he must gradually make away with all these malcontents, until he has

[3] *Ibid.*, p. 289.
[4] *Ibid.*, p. 293.

not a friend or an enemy left who is of any account." [5] The best elements in society are purged until all who are courageous, high-
minded, and intelligent are either killed or silenced. "The people
. . . have escaped the smoke only to fall into the fire, exchanging
service to free men for the tyranny of slaves. That freedom which
knew no bounds must now put on the livery of the most harsh and
bitter servitude, where the slave has become the master." [6] Freedom
conceived as license leads to anarchy, and anarchy manifests itself
politically in tyranny.

II

True freedom requires both knowledge of the good and the
will to choose the good when known. The denial of either is a denial
of freedom, and the denial of freedom is the rejection of that moral
agency in man which characterizes his humanity. In one of the best
analyses of the rise of National Socialism in Germany, Helmut Kuhn
explains the acceptance of Hitler as being made possible by a "flight
from freedom into forgetfulness." "Freedom," he says, "is rational
choice."

> The flight from freedom into forgetfulness presented itself,
> within the rarefied atmosphere of abstract thought, as a dialectic
> through which Reason was divorced from Choice. The Histori-
> cist, fastening on understanding to the exclusion of choice,
> reduced the mind to an impotent spectator. The Existentialist,
> exalting choice at the expense of reason, entrusted the self with
> a blind power of decision, thus reducing it to an irresponsible
> agent. After whittling away freedom from both ends, the two
> found themselves united in the task of consecrating the unfree-
> dom of the totalitarian state. A pre-established harmony obtained
> between their joint teaching on the one hand and the behavior

[5] *Ibid.*, p. 293.

[6] *Ibid.*, p. 296. A great deal of nonsense is written about Plato today, and much
of his thinking is presented in a distorted form to modern readers. A recent
example of this kind of distortion is K. R. Popper's *The Open Society and Its
Enemies* (London, 1945). An excellent answer to Popper's arguments will be
found in Robert Jordan's "The Revolt against Philosophy: The Spell of Popper,"
in John Wild (ed.), *The Return to Reason* (Chicago, 1953), and in John Wild's
Plato's Modern Enemies and the Theory of Natural Law (Chicago, 1953).

which the Third Reich expected from its citizens on the other. The required attitude combined the passivity of the spectator with the blind spontaneity of the unreasoning agent.[7]

The preservation of freedom demands that we recover our faith both in the ability of man to know the good and in his capacity, within the limitations of historical conditioning and the defectiveness of his will, to choose the good when known. That he will inevitably fall short of knowing the good in its completeness and of acting upon it unselfishly in every instance—so much we must concede to the intellectual and moral frailty of human nature—but only in the ever constant effort to transcend his limitations with the help of God can man's freedom be preserved and enlarged. When we talk today about the preservation of democracy, what most of us, I think, are concerned about is the preservation of freedom. We realize that democratic forms and institutions find their essential and ultimate meaning in the preservation and enlargement of human freedom. They are not ends in themselves but means to an ultimate end. They are not identical with freedom but the means through which freedom may find its best political expression.

Plato believed that in the ideal state political power and love of the good would be combined in the same individuals. This is the essential meaning of his declaration that in the ideal state philosophers will be kings, and kings philosophers. He meant by "philosophers" lovers of wisdom, seekers after the good. Whereas Plato, however, believed that only a few members of society could ever aspire to a life of virtue, it is the faith underlying modern democracy that all men may aspire to that life of virtue which Plato would restrict to the few.

That faith has a long and ancient lineage. It is probably first suggested by the Stoics and finds explicit expression in the writings of Cicero. "There is no human being of any race," writes Cicero, "who, if he finds a guide, cannot attain to virtue." [8] Men, he argues, are more alike than they are different, and between man and man there is no difference in kind. The distinguishing characteristic of man is

---

[7] *Freedom: Forgotten and Remembered* (Chapel Hill, 1943), p. 25. Quoted with permission of the University of North Carolina Press.

[8] *Laws* i. 10. 30, trans. Clinton W. Keyes (Loeb ed.; London, 1928).

his ability to reason, and it is this reason which links one man to another. Men attain virtue by following the principles of that law which "the gods have given to the human race." "Law is not a product of human thought, nor is it any enactment of peoples, but something eternal which rules thew hole universe by its wisdom in command and prohibition. . . . Law is the primal and ultimate mind of God whose reason directs all things either by compulsion or restraint." [9] In a celebrated passage in the *Republic*, Cicero declares:

> . . . True law is right reason in agreement with nature; it is of universal application, unchanging and everlasting; it summons to duty by its commands, and averts from wrongdoing by its prohibitions. And it does not lay its commands or prohibitions upon good men in vain, though neither have any effect on the wicked. It is a sin to try to alter this law, nor is it allowable to attempt to repeal any part of it, and it is impossible to abolish it entirely. We cannot be freed from its obligations by senate or people, and we need not look outside ourselves for an expounder or interpreter of it. And there will not be different laws at Rome and at Athens, or different laws now and in the future, but one eternal and unchangeable law will be valid for all nations and all times, and there will be one master and ruler, that is, God, over us all, for he is the author of this law, its promulgator and its enforcing judge. Whoever is disobedient is fleeing from himself and denying his human nature, and by reason of this very fact he will suffer the worst penalties, even if he escapes what is commonly considered punishment.[10]

It is in the light of this law that all men are equal—equal not in wealth, in talents, in physical strength or learning but equal in the capacity to distinguish justice from injustice, right from wrong. And it is this capacity, guided by the law of nature, that makes possible to all men equally the life of virtue which Plato thought possible only for the few. And it is these two doctrines—the doctrine of natural law and the equality of men—which lie at the foundation of what today we call "democracy" and which sharply distinguish it from the totalitarian systems.

[9] *Ibid.* ii. 4. 8.
[10] *Republic* iii. 22, trans. Clinton W. Keyes (Loeb ed.; London, 1928).

The Stoic conception of natural law is transmitted to the Middle Ages and from the Middle Ages to modern times through the teachings of Christianity, which retain the Stoic conception but identify it more explicitly as an expression of the eternal law of God. Christianity also teaches that a portion of that eternal law is revealed to men directly by God in the Divine Law, which both confirms and supplements the natural law of reason. This Divine Law is revealed in the Old Testament in the Ten Commandments which God gave to Moses and in the New by the commandment of Christ that we should love one another. The commandment that we should love one another does not abrogate the injunction of the natural law that we should render unto each man his due, but goes beyond it. And there is ascribed to the natural law a function not clearly perceived by the Stoics, namely, preparation through a life of virtue for a life eternal.

While the Stoic proclamation of a natural law emphasized the capacity of men to distinguish right from wrong, it also had the practical effect of emphasizing the inability of men to attain moral perfection through their own efforts. And men found themselves crying out in despair with Paul: "The good that I would, I do not, but the evil which I would not, that I do." And Christianity taught men that only through the love of God, through the reorientation of one's thoughts and action from self to God, through the submission of one's will to the will of God, could one hope to fulfil the law of God in its completeness. This is what Augustine meant when he said: "The law was therefore given, in order that grace might be sought; grace was given, in order that the law might be fulfilled." [11] And, again, "Our will is by the law shown to be weak, that grace may heal its infirmity." [12] Where Augustine, however, tended to emphasize the great disparity between nature and grace, later Christian thinkers, and notably Thomas Aquinas, argued that "grace does not annul nature but perfects it." The defect of man lies not in his reason but in his will.

Christianity does not deny the wisdom of the Stoics but incorporates it in its own teaching and adds to it. Augustine points out that

[11] *On the Spirit and the Letter*, Book XXXIV, in Whitney I. Oates (ed.), *Basic Writings of Saint Augustine* (2 vols.; New York, 1948), I, 487.
[12] *Ibid.* Book XV, in Oates, *op. cit.*, I, 472.

man is not simply a citizen of this world but a pilgrim seeking the Kingdom of God. "Two cities," he says, "have been formed by two loves: the earthly by the love of self, even to the contempt of God; the heavenly by the love of God, even to the contempt of self . . . the one seeks glory from men; but the greatest glory of the other is God, the witness of conscience." [13] The Kingdom of God is above all states, races, and classes and knows neither free man nor slave, Gentile nor Jew, male nor female. It is a universal community of persons bound together by mutual love and the love of God. The Stoic conception of equality is not denied but is given a spiritual content and meaning which it lacked. Absolute justice and perfect peace are found only in this kingdom, where love rules supreme. All earthly kingdoms, due to the defective will of man, necessarily fall short of this perfection. The peace and justice at which earthly kingdoms aim are good but only relatively good, for the peace and justice at which they aim, while essential to the attainment of everlasting peace and perfect justice, are not identical with them. Men owe allegiance to civil society; but, because they have an ultimate destiny that transcends life on earth, they have a greater obligation and a greater allegiance, namely, an allegiance to God.

The effect of this teaching is not only to distinguish the secular from the spiritual spheres but to place the secular authority under the sanction of a higher authority. And the life of wisdom and virtue, which Plato thought possible only for a few, is now conceived as being available through the grace of God to all men equally. And this has important consequences for politics. For if there is an authority higher than the authority of any particular state, then no state can demand our absolute obedience or attempt to control every aspect of our lives. This is the issue which sharply separates the totalitarian states in the modern world from the democracies. The totalitarian state is made possible only by the denial of a higher allegiance, and its totalitarian character arises from a refusal to acknowledge the existence of a sphere of human life over which no political control may legitimately be exercised. Democracies recognize that there are aspects of human life which the state may not legitimately control; and that recognition has its roots, when it is recognized, in the teach-

[13] *City of God* xiv. 28, in Oates, *op. cit.*, II, 274.

ings of the Christian religion. Above the authority of the state, there is the authority of God, and this is precisely what the totalitarian states refuse to acknowledge. The authority of God may be conceived as mediated by the church or as communicated directly to the private conscience of the individual; but the form in which the authority of God is recognized is less important than is the recognition of that authority itself.

Freedom and authority are often thought of today as being in opposition to one another, and we frequently hear the modern dictatorships referred to as "authoritarian." Now authority means the right to enforce obedience, but it is precisely the unwillingness of dictators like Hitler and Stalin to feel any necessity for justifying their power that is characteristic of their rule. They deny that anyone may question their right to rule, indeed, deny that there is any authority or any standard of right in terms of which their actions may be evaluated.

The totalitarian dictatorship is the embodiment not of authority but of naked power—it repudiates the demands of reason, justice, and God. It is an effort to fill the void left by the repudiation of reason and of God by a will that is unguided by reason, unrestrained by considerations of justice, and unmindful of the commandments of God. It is not government in the true sense of the word but a perverted attempt to employ the techniques of government when government fails. The total character of the dictatorship is necessitated by the *lack* of any common authority. Compulsion replaces consent in every sphere of life, because there is no longer any common agreement obliging consent in any sphere. No authority exists to which an appeal can be taken. The will of the tyrant is the final court of appeal, and that will is a purely arbitrary one. It is useless to appeal to the tyrant's reason or sense of justice, for the tyrant denies that he must justify his actions in terms of reason or of justice. It is enough that he has commanded an action—the rightfulness of his command is not subject to debate, and it may not be questioned. And it was the positivist jurists who proclaimed that law is nothing but the will of the ruling power who prepared the way for this tyranny. Emil Brunner has said: "The totalitarian state is simply and solely legal positivism in political practice, the abrogation in actual fact of the classical and Christian idea of a divine 'law of nature.' . . . If there is no justice transcending the state, then the state can declare anything it likes to be law; there is no limit set to its arbitrariness save its actual power to give force to its will. If it does so in the form of a logically coherent system, it thereby fulfills the one condition to which the legality of law is bound in the formalistic view of law. The totalitarian state is the inevitable result of the slow disintegration of the idea of justice in the Western world." The totalitarian state, Brunner points out, is not a criminal conspiracy but the product of the Western world's own thinking, "the ineluctable consequence of its own positivism, a positivism void of faith and inimical to metaphysics and religion." [14]

It is not a characteristic feature of democracy that it dispenses with authority; that is, instead, characteristic of tyranny. There can be no freedom without authority, for without authority freedom degenerates into license. The state of anarchy which Plato describes as preceding the rise of tyranny is characterized by the lack of any order in individual and social life, by the lack of rational restraint. And it is within

[14] *Justice and the Social Order* (New York: Harper & Row, 1945), pp. 7-8. Brunner describes the disintegration of the idea of justice in this way: "Its disintegration set in with the Age of Reason. Firstly, the *divine* law of nature, the objective, super-human standard of justice, became the subjective law of human reason, its substance soon being narrowed down into the individualistic notion of subjective rights of man. Later, following the trend of the time, the element of 'nature' in law was reinterpreted in a naturalistic sense. The historicism of the Romantic period then declared war on a timelessly valid justice, replacing it by the conception of justice as a historical growth. It was, however, the positivism of the nineteenth century, with its denial of the metaphysical and superhuman, which dissolved the idea of justice by proclaiming the relativity of all views of justice. Thereby the idea of justice was stripped of all divine dignity and law abandoned to the vagaries of human will. The view that justice is of its nature relative became the dogma of the jurists, and the proof seemed to lie at hand in the concrete facts of history. Men ceased to believe in an eternal standard of justice transcending all human legislation; the difference between right and wrong became a convention, law was conceived as the mere product of the reigning power. Finally the idea of justice was reduced to a mere husk by the complete codification of law at the beginning of the nineteenth century, after which it meant nothing more than the demand for a system of law without contradiction in form, but without any value as a criterion in substance.

"Hence it was only to be expected that one day a political power devoid of all religious scruples should discard the last vestiges of the traditional idea of justice and proclaim the will of the ruling power as the sole canon of appeal in matters of law" (*ibid.*, pp. 6-7). Quoted with permission of Harper & Row.

the framework of rational restraint that the democratic principle of majority rule is to be understood.

III

It is an accepted and distinguishing principle of democratic government that, as John Locke put it, "the majority have a right to act and conclude the rest." Unanimity of judgment is never possible; and if action is to be taken, it cannot wait for unanimity. The closer the judgments of the people approximate unanimity, the greater the degree of consent secured for any action or policy; but no government could ever operate upon the principle of unanimity. How, then, are we to conceive of rule by the majority of the people? Does it mean, as some contend, that the will of the majority is to be regarded as sovereign, that there is no appeal from that will, that its judgment is absolute and unlimited? Is the rightness or wisdom of governmental policy to be determined solely by the counting of votes? Does the principle of majority rule demand that we abandon all qualitative judgments in favor of a quantitative method? I do not think so, and I think it would be dangerous to insist that it does. If the principle of majority rule means that the will of the majority must be conceived as unlimited and absolute, then it is a principle, as the framers of our Constitution realized, that is indistinguishable from tyranny. For the essence of tyranny is unrestrained will—whether it be the will of one man, of several, or of many. And the tyranny of a majority is no less cruel or unjust—indeed, may be more so—than the tyranny of a single individual. How, then, are we to conceive of rule by the majority of the people?

What is demanded by the democratic form of government is not submission to the will of the majority because that will is numerically superior but rather submission to the reasoned judgment of the majority. We are obligated to submit to the decision of the majority, not because that decision represents a numerically superior will, but because it represents the best judgment of society with respect to a particular matter at a particular time. It is founded not upon the principle that the will of the many should prevail over the will of the few but rather upon the principle that the judgment of the many is likely to be superior to the judgment of the few. "For the many," as Aristotle declared, "of whom each individual is but an ordinary person, when they meet together may very likely be better than the few good, if regarded not individually but collectively. . . . For each individual among the many has a share of virtue and prudence, and when they meet together, they become in a manner one man, who has many feet, and hands, and senses; that is a figure of their mind and disposition. Hence the many are better judges than a single man . . . for some understand one part, and some another, and among them they understand the whole." [15] The principle of majority rule is founded upon the belief that the widest possible popular discussion and participation in the formulation of policy is likely to yield wiser decisions than a discussion limited to the few. The decision recorded by majority vote may then be fairly said to represent not a portion of society but the whole people.

And discussion and deliberation in a democracy are conceived as being continuous. While a majority vote is necessary in order temporarily to conclude a discussion and reach a decision, that decision remains open for discussion, and no decision is regarded as irrevocable. It always remains revocable in the sense that the minority is always free to continue the discussion and to endeavor to persuade others of the wisdom of its reasoning. The majority is not composed always of the same persons but it is a fluctuating one, and the possibility always remains open for the minority to become the majority through the instruments of persuasion.

The majority vote does not precede the discussion but concludes it; it is the recording of a decision reached through deliberation and is not conceived to take the place of deliberation. To the extent that the discussion is not as widespread as possible, to the extent that judgment is coerced rather than persuaded, to the extent that the discussion is not carried on in as reasonable a manner as is possible, to the extent that it is used to obscure issues rather than to clarify them, to the extent that the participants make no effort to transcend the motivations of their private interests to contemplate the common good—to that extent the principle of majority rule is corrupted and debased. It is the reasoned judgment of the majority that obliges our

[15] *Politics* iii. 11. 2-3.

compliance with its decision, not the will of the majority as such. To the degree, therefore, that rule by the majority becomes more an expression of will and less an expression of reasoned judgment, to that degree does it become less democratic and more tyrannical.

The democratic process is designed to determine by popular discussion and decision the choice of the best means to achieve the common good. In a recent discussion of the philosophy of democratic government, Professor Yves Simon has said:

> In essence, deliberation is about means and presupposes that the problem of ends has been settled. In the order of action, propositions relative to ends have the character of principles; they are anterior to deliberation and presupposed by it. The freedom of expression which is required by the democratic process of persuasion concerns all subjects that have the character of means and are matters of deliberation. Under fully normal circumstances the propositions relative to the very ends of social life are above deliberation in democracy as well as in any other system. Circumstances which make it necessary to deliver the principles of a society, its very soul, to the hazards of controversy are a fateful threat to any regime, democratic or not.[16]

He goes on to say that "a democracy may have to allow the questioning of the most indispensable principles" but such questioning is a grave sign of weakness and may point to the eventual disintegration of that society. "In democracy more than in any other regime it is a problem to assert principles in such a way as not to jeopardize the free discussion of means, and to insure free discussion of means without jeopardizing the principles without which social life no longer has end or form. The risks proper to democratic practice demand that the assertion of principles be more profound, more vital, and more heartfelt than elsewhere. Unless this assertion is embodied in the living essence of community life, it will be nonexistent." [17]

Admittedly, the discussion in a democracy will never be completely rational, and private interests will always intrude themselves into any

[16] *Philosophy of Democratic Government* (Chicago, 1951), p. 123. Quoted with permission of the University of Chicago Press.
[17] *Ibid.*, p. 124.

discussion of the common good; but a sound democracy will aim at achieving as rational a discussion as is humanly possible and at subordinating private interests as much as possible to the common good. This demands considerable self-discipline of both an intellectual and a moral character on the part of the individuals who compose the democratic society. It is the faith that such self-discipline is possible that makes democracy preferable to other forms of government that would restrict government to the few. The self-discipline that we expect of the adult in a democratic society has its roots in the early training of the child; and the kind of education, therefore, that we give our children, both at home and in school, may well determine the possibility or impossibility of democracy. The self-restraint that the adult must practice if democracy is not to degenerate into anarchy must grow out of the habits acquired in childhood. A child that knows no restraints, upon whom no discipline is imposed, is likely to grow into an adult who chafes at restraints and who is incapable of self-discipline.

Initially, the responsibility for developing good character rests with parents, for it is by virtue of their authority, which they may choose or not choose to exercise, that good habits are encouraged and bad ones discouraged. Virtue is acquired by the repeated performance of virtuous acts, and initially these acts must be compelled under authority. Not only will parents inculcate good habits of conduct, but they will encourage the habit of deliberation before action, and through formal education the rational faculty of deliberation will be trained to recognize the means by which human nature is perfected. This means that children must be taught the precepts of the natural or moral law much as we now teach the fundamentals of arithmetic or the rules of English grammar. If self-discipline is as essential to the preservation of freedom in a democratic society as is literacy, we shall not neglect the inculcation of moral principles any more than we would neglect to teach our children to read and to write. John Middleton Murry has said:

> Just as the democratic society freely chooses its government, so the democratic citizen must freely choose to do his duty to the commonweal. He puts his conscience in control of his actions. He obeys the law, not as an external command, but as the ex-

pression of his own better self, which wills to act in obedience to a law which its reason recognizes to be necessary. . . . Democracy is based not only in theory but in fact upon the reality of a universal obligation to obey the moral law. If that obligation is not recognized, and acted on, democracy must, in time of real stress, collapse. If the validity of the moral law is an illusion, so is the validity of democracy.[18]

But if we recognize the necessity for individuals in a democracy to strive to bring their thoughts and actions under the guidance of the moral law, we must not overlook the fact that the inherent defect of the human will to some extent will always thwart that endeavor. We must keep a balance between an excessive optimism about the motives of men and an excessive pessimism about their potentialities. Reinhold Niebuhr has written:

> A free society requires some confidence in the ability of men to reach tentative and tolerable adjustments between their competing interests and to arrive at some common notions of justice which transcend all partial interests. A consistent pessimism in regard to man's rational capacity for justice leads to absolutistic political theories; for they prompt the conviction that only preponderant power can coerce the various vitalities of a community into a working harmony. But a too consistent optimism in regard to man's ability and inclination to grant justice to his fellows obscures the perils of chaos which perennially confront every society, including a free society. . . . If these perils are not appreciated they may overtake a free society and invite the alternative evil of tyranny.

He suggests that it is "man's capacity for justice" which "makes democracy possible" and "man's inclination to injustice" which "makes democracy necessary." [19]

This is a very useful formula for understanding democracy, and it is one, I think, that the framers of our Constitution would have understood and approved. And none understood it any better than

[18] "The Moral Foundations of Democracy," *Fortnightly* (September 1947), p. 168.

[19] *The Children of Light and the Children of Darkness* (New York, 1944), pp. x-xi. Quoted with permission of Charles Scribner's Sons.

John Adams. Commenting upon the statement that "the people never think of usurping over other men's rights," Adams declares:

> Is not a great part, I will not say the greatest part, of men detected every day in some disposition or other, stronger or weaker, more or less, to usurp over other men's rights? There are some few, indeed, whose whole lives and conversations show that in every thought, word, and action, they conscientiously respect the rights of others. There is a larger body still, who, in the general tenor of their thoughts and actions, discover similar principles and feelings, yet frequently err. If we should extend our candor so far as to own, that the majority of men are generally under the dominion of benevolence and good intentions, yet, it must be confessed, that a vast majority frequently transgress; and, what is more directly to the point, not only a majority, but almost all, confine their benevolence to their families, relations, personal friends, parish, village, city, county, province, and that very few, indeed, extend it impartially to the whole community. Now, grant but this truth and the question is decided. If a majority are capable of preferring their own private interest, or that of their families, counties, and party, to that of the nation collectively, some provision must be made in the constitution, in favor of justice, to compel all to respect the common right, the public good, the universal law, in preference to all private and partial considerations.[20]

"Self-interest," he goes on to say, "private avidity, ambition, and avarice, will exist in every state of society, and under every form of government." Since they cannot be eliminated, it is necessary to control their effects. The only remedy is so to divide power that the selfishness of one group will check the selfishness of another and no one group, minority or majority, will have sufficient power to tyrannize the rest. The principle of the separation of powers, with its attendant system of checks and balances; the principle of federalism, with the division of power upon a geographical basis, were all designed by the framers of our Constitution to preserve liberty by making the concentration of political power in the hands of a few

[20] John Adams, A *Defence of the Constitutions of Government of the United States of America* (3 vols.; London, 1787-88), III, 215-16.

or of many a difficult, if not an impossible, undertaking. To this extent they realized that it is man's inclination to injustice that makes democracy necessary. The widespread diffusion of power is essential if that power is not to be abused. At the same time, they recognized that government exists to promote justice—in the words of Adams "to compel all to respect the common right, the public good, the universal law, in preference to all private and partial considerations." And it is this capacity of men to respect the common right, the public good, and the universal law, though they often need the compulsion of law to implement that respect, that makes democracy possible.

Under the influence of liberalism we undoubtedly developed too sanguine a view of the natural impulse of men to do good and consequently were plunged into despair when the liberal view of men was proved, by the force of events, to be too optimistic. In reaction to that view of man we have now come under the tutelage of historical events to a more realistic understanding of man's propensity to do evil. Woodrow Wilson's hope that the world could be made "safe for democracy" seems now to have been naïve, though it did not appear so then; and in reaction to that optimism many persons now proclaim that the only reality in international politics is power and the self-interest of nations. Many intellectuals today not only underestimate the power of moral ideals but deny that moral ideals have any other role to play than that of rationalizing our private and selfish interests.

This reaction, however, may prove as devastating in its effects as was the liberal optimism from which it is the reaction. In correcting the errors in the liberal view of man, we must not discard the truth as well. To recognize the propensity in human nature to do evil is essential if we are to be realistic in dealing with the political and social problems that confront us; but if the recognition of the evil in man is proclaimed to be the whole wisdom about man, it will lead us to despair of man and to finding proximate solutions to our problems. A view of man that regards him as totally depraved is as one-sided and distorted as is the view which regards him as completely well-intentioned. A balanced view of man will emphasize both his propensity to do evil and his capacity to do good; it will not overestimate his motives, but it will not underestimate his potentialities. *Recogni-*

tion of the sinfulness of human nature was never intended to paralyze man's capacity for intelligent thought and moral action but to liberate that capacity in the service of God rather than of self. A balanced view of man will recognize the necessity for institutional checks upon the abuse of power, the necessity for law and coercion to restrain men from evil actions; but it will also understand that men are naturally attracted to the good, and it will seek to foster and develop this natural capacity. A balanced view of man will save us from the illusion that we can establish a political or social system which is perfect or make a reform which is final; but it will not despair of man's capacity for justice, and it will appeal to that capacity in seeking social change.

The degradation of man is amply attested to by the events of our time; and while we must be realistic in identifying the source of that degradation, the rebellious will of man, we require no lessons in despair. We know full well the depths to which men can sink. What we need to remind ourselves of are the heights to which men may climb. Under the influence of liberalism and the philosophy of the Enlightenment we believed that men could climb those heights alone and unassisted. That belief has now been shattered by the force of historical events. And many men, as a consequence, have been plunged into cynical despair. But we need not disparage the attractiveness of the heights or despair of men's approaching them if we remind ourselves of something the Age of Enlightenment forgot—that man is not an autonomous being but the creature of God, his moral weakness is his own, but his moral strength is born of the love of God. What the modern world has almost forgotten is the reality of spirit and its power; and history shows that it is the power of spirit that ultimately triumphs over material power, however great or formidable. The greatest empires and the worst tyrannies have ultimately come to an end, but the spirit of man has risen each time from their ruins to begin again the work of reconstruction. A contemporary writer has defined spirit as "the creative activity by which persons apprehend universal truth and good with rational insight and serve men with love born of faith in their divine potentialities." [21]

---

[21] George F. Thomas, *Spirit and Its Freedom* (Chapel Hill, 1939), p. 69. Quoted with permission of the University of North Carolina Press.

This is the kind of spirit that has risen triumphant before in history and will again.

Democracy rests upon a faith in man as a rational, moral, and spiritual creature, and it is as much aspiration as it is fact. The ideals of democracy never have been and never will be achieved with perfection—they are goals constantly to be striven for but never perfectly realized. In the last analysis, democracy is "a venture of faith in the moral and spiritual possibilities of men when entrusted with freedom." [22] Whether that freedom will be used to promote a just social order in which the moral and spiritual potentialities of all men equally will be encouraged to grow or whether it will degenerate into license and anarchy depends upon how each one of us conceives and uses it.

IV

Running throughout the history of Western thought there can be traced, broadly speaking, two competing conceptions of freedom, two competing philosophies of life. These two conceptions are represented in one of the Platonic dialogues by Callicles, on the one hand, and Socrates, on the other.[23] But each has had its counterpart in the life and literature of the Western world since that time, and the debate is one that continues in our own day. One regards freedom as the power to do what one wants; the other regards freedom as service to God and one's fellow-men. One regards power as an end in itself; the other as a means to promote justice and the common good.

The good, Callicles argues, is the gratification of desire, the pursuit of pleasure, and "he who would truly live ought to allow his desires to wax to the uttermost, and not to chastise them; but when they have grown to their greatest he should have courage and intelligence to minister to them and to satisfy all their longings." It is because the many cannot attain to this life and because they are ashamed of their weakness that "they praise temperance and justice out of their own cowardice." The truly great and noble man is the one who lives by the law of nature, which decrees that the weakest shall go to the

[22] *Ibid.*, p. 147.
[23] *Gorgias.*

wall. Might makes right is the first law of nature, and no man or society can stand up against it. In "reality" the ugly thing is not to commit a wrong or an injustice but to suffer one. It is the weaklings who have to "put up" with wrongs; and if we look at things as they really are, we shall see that it is the strong who invariably push the weaker aside. The right of the strong to impose their will on the weak, although contrary to conventional morality, is the first principle of natural morality. Callicles is convinced that "superior ability of any kind gives the moral right to use the ability according to your own judgment and without scruples. Hence he feels that in rejecting 'conventionalism' in morals he is not rejecting morality itself; he is appealing from a petty and confined morality of local human conventions to an august morality of 'Nature' or 'things-as-they-are.' " [24]

Callicles prides himself on being a "realist" and "a man of the world." The world of politics and of business has no need or use for the philosopher. Philosophy is for children, not for men of the world. Indeed, says Callicles, if I should see a man continuing the study of philosophy "in later life, and not leaving off, I should like to beat him . . . for such a one, even though he have good natural parts, becomes effeminate. He flies from the busy center and the market place, in which . . . men become distinguished and he creeps into a corner for the rest of his life." The world of politics, Callicles insists, is in need not of moral principles but of aggressive men who know that justice is nothing more than the will of the stronger. Such is one conception of freedom, and it is by no means confined to Callicles or to the fifth century B.C.

Socrates replies to the argument of Callicles by pointing out that the pursuit of pleasure itself is an endless pursuit and that the sensual desires of men are insatiable. The more we satisfy our desires, the more they crave, and our souls become like leaking casks that can never be filled. The impossibility of satisfying our desires shows the absurdity of the attempt. It is not the satisfaction of all kinds of desire without limit that men really want but happiness; and how is happiness possible without some rational principle in terms of which we can differentiate good pleasures from bad? A man who does exactly as he pleases in response to the desires of the moment is not

[24] A. E. Taylor, *Plato: The Man and His Work* (New York, 1929), p. 116.

a free man or a happy one but a slave to his passions, miserable in his bondage. He cannot truly be said to do as he pleases, for what he pleases is not within his rational control. If he would pursue that which is truly good for him as a human being, he must have some rational understanding of that good and exercise rational restraint over his desires.

Freedom consists not in the pursuit of pleasure but in a disciplined, ordered life directed to the perfection of that which is distinctively human. There is a good of the soul, just as there is a good of the body, and there is a science appropriate to each. The good of the body we call health, and the science of health is the science of medicine. It is this standard of health which the physician tries to reproduce in his patients. Corresponding to the science of medicine, there is a moral science which is concerned with the health of the soul. Just as the physician aims to produce a definite "order and regulation" in a human body, so the statesman should aim at producing "temperance and justice" in the souls of the citizens. Politics is a practical art which demands a knowledge of human nature and that which is its distinctive good. Citizens are not things to be manipulated but persons embodying ends in themselves—to minister to those ends is the distinctive art of statesmanship. Just as the physician's art depends for its successful practice upon a knowledge of the rules of health, so the statesman's art depends upon a knowledge of moral principles.

Callicles may be right in thinking, says Socrates, that the rule of life which Socrates prescribes is liable to leave an individual at the mercy of an aggressor, but he is wrong in thinking that life [is] ugly. The "leviathan" says Callicles will kill you if you do not humor it. But Socrates replies that the important thing is not to live long but to live well. The dreadful thing is not to die but to enter the unseen world with a soul laden with guilt. No one, says Socrates, can escape Divine judgment, and before that judgment it is not the life prescribed by Socrates that will appear ugly but rather the way of life prescribed by Callicles.

Plato has described in the *Republic* how a society in which men allow their "desires to wax to the uttermost," who allow all desires free rein, at last succumb to a master-passion "as leader of the soul," which "takes madness for the captain of its guard and breaks out in frenzy." Tyranny, he shows us graphically, is the fruit of an undisciplined and disorderly life. Freedom conceived as the unrestrained pursuit of pleasure leads to slavery. The modern tyrants differ from the tyrants of Plato's day only by the fact that they have greater power at their disposal. They are not content to oppress men's bodies but endeavor by every modern technique of psychological coercion to coerce men's souls as well. "Under such circumstances the victory of Socrates over Callicles is not an academic question, it is a question of the life or death of modern civilization." [25]

[25] Thomas, *op. cit.,* p. 125.

III CRITERIA
OF INTERPRETATION

ON CLASSICAL POLITICAL
PHILOSOPHY   Leo Strauss

The purpose of the following remarks is to discuss especially those characteristic features of classical political philosophy which are in particular danger of being overlooked or insufficiently stressed by the schools that are most influential in our time. These remarks are not intended to sketch the outlines of an adequate interpretation of classical political philosophy. They will have fulfilled their purpose if they point to the way which, as it seems to me, is the only one whereby such an interpretation can eventually be reached by us.

Classical political philosophy is characterized by the fact that it was related to political life directly. It was only after the classical philosophers had done their work that political philosophy became definitely "established" and thus acquired a certain remoteness from political life. Since that time the relationship of political philosophers to political life, and their grasp of it, has been determined by the existence of an inherited political philosophy: since then political philosophy has been related to political life through the medium of a tradition of political philosophy. The tradition of political philosophy, being a tradition, took for granted the necessity and possibility of political philosophy. The tradition that originated in classical Greece was rejected in the sixteenth and seventeenth centuries in favor of a new political philosophy. But this "revolution" did not

Leo Strauss *is Robert Maynard Hutchins Distinguished Service Professor of Political Science, University of Chicago. "On Classical Political Philosophy" is an article from* Social Research, *vol. 12, no. 1 (February 1945), pp. 98-117. Copyright 1945 by the New School for Social Research. Reprinted by permission of* Social Research.

restore the direct relation to political life that had existed in the beginning: the new political philosophy was related to political life through the medium of the inherited general notion of political philosophy or political science, and through the medium of a new concept of science. The modern political philosophers tried to replace both the teaching and the method of traditional political philosophy by what they considered as the true teaching and the right method; they took it for granted that political philosophy as such is necessary and possible. Today, political science may believe that by rejecting or by emancipating itself from political philosophy, it stands in the most direct relation to political life; actually it is related to political life through the medium of modern natural science, or of the reaction to modern natural science, and through a number of basic concepts inherited from the philosophic tradition, however despised or ignored.

It was its direct relation to political life that determined the orientation and scope of classical political philosophy. Accordingly, the tradition which was based on that philosophy, and which preserved its orientation and scope, preserved that direct relation to a certain extent. The fundamental change in this respect begins with the new political philosophy of the early modern period and reaches its climax in present-day political science. The most striking difference between classical political philosophy and present-day political science is that the latter is no longer concerned at all with what was the guiding question for the former: the question of the best political order. On the other hand, modern political science is greatly preoccupied with a type of question that was of much less importance to classical political philosophy: questions concerning method. Both differences must be traced to the same reason: to the different degree of directness in which classical political philosophy, on the one hand, and present-day political science, on the other, are related to political life.

Classical political philosophy attempted to reach its goal by accepting the basic distinctions made in political life exactly in the sense and with the orientation in which they are made in political life, and by thinking them through, by understanding them as perfectly as possible. It did not start from such basic distinctions as those between "the state of nature" and "the civil state," between "facts" and "values," between "reality" and "ideologies," between "the world" and "the worlds" of different societies, or between "the I, Me, Thou, and We," distinctions which are alien, and even unknown, to political life as such and which originate only in philosophic or scientific reflection. Nor did it try to bring order into that chaos of political "facts" which exists only for those who approach political life from a point of view outside of political life, that is to say, from the point of view of a science that is not itself essentially an element of political life. Instead, it followed carefully and even scrupulously the articulation which is inherent in, and natural to, political life and its objectives.

The primary questions of classical political philosophy, and the terms in which it stated them, were not specifically philosophic or scientific; they were questions that are raised in assemblies, councils, clubs, and cabinets, and they were stated in terms intelligible and familiar, at least to all sane adults, from everyday experience and everyday usage. These questions have a natural hierarchy which supplies political life, and hence political philosophy, with its fundamental orientation. No one can help distinguishing among questions of smaller, of greater, and of paramount importance, and between questions of the moment and questions that are always present in political communities; and intelligent men apply these distinctions intelligently.

Similarly it can be said that the method, too, of classical political philosophy was presented by political life itself. Political life is characterized by conflicts between men asserting opposed claims. Those who raise a claim usually believe that what they claim is good for them. In many cases they believe, and in most cases they say, that what they claim is good for the community at large. In almost all cases claims are raised, sometimes sincerely and sometimes insincerely, in the name of justice. The opposed claims are based, then, on opinions of what is good or just. To justify their claims, the opposed parties advance arguments. The conflict calls for arbitration, for an intelligent decision that will give each party what it truly deserves. Some of the material required for making such a decision is offered by the opposed parties themselves, and the very insufficiency of this partial material—an insufficiency obviously due to its partisan origin—points the way to its completion by the umpire. The umpire par excellence is the political philosopher.[1] He tries to settle those political controversies that are both of paramount and of permanent importance.

This view of the function of the political philosopher—that he must not be a "radical" partisan who prefers victory in civil war to arbitration—is also of political origin: it is the duty of the good citizen to make civil strife cease and to create, by persuasion, agreement among the citizens.[2] The political philosopher first comes into sight as a good citizen who can perform this function of the good citizen in the best way and on the highest level. In order to perform his function he has to raise ulterior questions, questions that are never raised in the political arena; but in doing so he does not abandon his fundamental orientation, which is the orientation inherent in political life. Only if that orientation were abandoned, if the basic distinctions made by political life were considered merely "subjective" or "unscientific" and therefore disregarded, would the question of how to approach political things in order to understand them, that is to say, the question of method, become a fundamental question, and, indeed, *the* fundamental question.

It is true that political life is concerned primarily with the individual community to which the people happen to belong, and mostly even with individual situations, whereas political philosophy is concerned primarily with what is essential to all political communities. Yet there is a straight and almost continuous way leading from the prephilosophic to the philosophic approach. Political life requires various kinds of skills, and in particular that apparently highest skill which enables a man to manage well the affairs of his political community as a whole. That skill—the art, the prudence, the practical wisdom, the specific understanding possessed by the excellent statesman or politician—and not "a body of true propositions" con-

[1] Note the procedure of Aristotle in *Politics*, 1280a7-1284b34 and 1297a6-7; also Plato, *Eighth Letter*, 354al-5 and 352c8 ff., and Laws, 627dll-628a4.

[2] See Xenophon, *Memorabilia*, IV 6, 14-15 and context; also Aristotle, *Athenian Constitution*, 28, 5; also the remark by Hume (in his essay "Of the Original Contract"): "But philosophers, who have embraced a party (if that be not a contradiction in terms). . . ." The difference between the classical political philosopher and the present day political scientists is illustrated by Macaulay's remark on Sir William Temple: "Temple was not a mediator. He was merely a neutral." Cf. de Tocqueville, *De la démocratie en Amérique*: "J'ai entrepris de voir, non pas autrement, mais plus loin que les partis."

cerning political matters which is transmitted by teachers to pupils, is what was originally meant by "political science." A man who possesses "political science" is not merely able to deal properly with a large variety of situations in his own community; he can, in principle, manage well even the affairs of any other political community, be it "Greek" or "barbarian." While all political life is essentially the life of this or that political community, "political science," which essentially belongs to political life, is essentially "transferable" from one community to any other. A man like Themistocles was admired and listened to not only in Athens, but, after he had to flee from Athens, among the barbarians as well; such a man is admired because he is capable of giving sound political advice wherever he goes.[3]

"Political science" designated originally the skill by virtue of which a man could manage well the affairs of political communities by deed and by speech. The skill of speaking takes precedence over the skill of doing since all sensible action proceeds from deliberation, and the element of deliberation is speech. Accordingly, that part of political skill which first became the object of instruction was the skill of public speaking. "Political science" in a more precise sense, that is, as a skill that is essentially teachable, appeared first as rhetoric, or as a part of it. The teacher of rhetoric was not necessarily a politician or statesman; he was, however, a teacher of politicians or statesmen. Since his pupils belonged to the most different political communities, the content of his teaching could not possibly be bound up with the particular features of any individual political community. "Political science," on the level which it reached as a result of the exertions of the rhetoricians, is more "universal," is to an even higher degree "transferable," than is "political science" as the skill of the excellent statesman or politician: whereas strangers as statesmen or political advisers were an exception, strangers as teachers of rhetoric were the rule.[4]

[3] Xenophon, *Memorabilia*, III 6, 2; Thucydides, I 138. See also Plato, *Lysis*, 209d5-210b2, and *Republic*, 494c7-d1. One of the purposes of the *Menexenus* is to illustrate the "transferable" character of political science: a sufficiently gifted foreign woman is as capable as Pericles, or more capable than he, to compose a most solemn speech to be delivered on behalf of the city of Athens.

[4] Plato, *Protagoras*, 319a1-2, and *Timaeus*, 19e; also Aristotle, *Nicomachean Ethics*, 1181a12 ff. as well as *Politics*, 1264b33-34 and 1299a1-2; Isocrates, *To Nicocles* 9; Cicero, *De oratore*, III, 57.

Classical political philosophy rejected the identification of political science with rhetoric; it held that rhetoric, at its best, was only an instrument of political science. It did not, however, descend from the level of generality that had been reached by the rhetoricians. On the contrary, after that part of political skill which is the skill of speaking had been raised to the level of a distinct discipline, the classical philosophers could meet that challenge only by raising the whole of "political science," as far as possible or necessary, to the rank of a distinct discipline. By doing this they became the founders of political science in the precise and final sense of the term. And the way in which they did it was determined by the articulation natural to the political sphere.

"Political science" as the skill of the excellent politician or states-man consists in the right handling of individual situations; its immediate "products" are commands or decrees or advices effectively expressed, which are intended to cope with an individual case. Political life knows, however, a still higher kind of political understanding, which is concerned not with individual cases but, as regards each relevant subject, with all cases, and whose immediate "products"—laws and institutions—are meant to be permanent. The true legisla-tors—"the fathers of the Constitution," as modern men would say—establish, as it were, the permanent framework within which the right handling of changing situations by excellent politicians or states-men can take place. While it is true that the excellent statesman can act successfully within the most different frameworks of laws and institutions, the value of his achievement depends ultimately on the value of the cause in whose service he acts; and that cause is not his work but the work of him or those who made the laws and institu-tions of his community. The legislative skill is, therefore, the most "architectonic" political skill [5] that is known to political life.

Every legislator is primarily concerned with the individual com-munity for which he legislates, but he has to raise certain questions which regard all legislation. These most fundamental and most uni-

---

[5] Aristotle, *Nicomachean Ethics*, 1141b24-29 (compare 1137b13); also Plato, *Gorgias*, 464b7-8, and *Minos*, 320c1-5; Cicero, *Offices*, I, 75-76. The classical view was expressed as follows by Rousseau, who still shared it, or rather restored it: "s'il est vrai qu'un grand prince est un homme rare, que sera-ce d'un grand législateur? Le premier n'a qu'à suivre le modèle que l'autre doit proposer" (*Contrat social*, II, 7).

versal political questions are naturally fit to be made the subject of the most "architectonic," the truly "architectonic" political knowledge: of that political science which is the goal of the political philosopher. This political science is the knowledge which would enable a man to teach legislators. The political philosopher who has reached his goal is the teacher of legislators.[6] The knowledge of the political philosopher is "transferable" in the highest degree. Plato demonstrated this *ad oculos* in his dialogue on legislation, by presenting in the guise of a stranger the philosopher who is a teacher of legislators.[7] He illustrated it less ambiguously by the comparison, which frequently occurs in his writings, of political science with medicine.

It is by being the teacher of legislators that the political philosopher is the umpire par excellence. All political conflicts that arise within the community are at least related to, if they do not proceed from, the most fundamental political controversy: the controversy as to what type of men should rule the community. And the right settlement of that controversy appears to be the basis of excellent legislation.

Classical political philosophy was related to political life directly, because its guiding subject was a subject of actual political controversy carried on in pre-philosophic political life. Since all political controversies presuppose the existence of the political community, the classics are not primarily concerned with the question of whether and why there is, or should be, a political community; hence the question of the nature and purpose of the political community is not the guiding question for classical political philosophy. Similarly, to question the desirability or necessity of the survival and independence of one's political community normally means to commit the crime of treason; in other words, the ultimate aim of foreign policy is not essentially controversial. Hence classical political philosophy is not

[6] Consider Plato, *Laws*, 630b8-c4 and 631d-632d, and Aristotle, *Nicomachean Ethics*, 1180a33 ff. and 1109b34 ff. as well as *Politics*, 1297b37-38; cf. Isocrates, *To Nicocles* 6 and Montesquieu, *Esprit des Lois*, beginning of the 29th book. On the difference between political science proper and political skill see Thomas Aquinas' commentary on Aristotle's *Ethics*, VI, lectio 7, and also Fārābī's *Enumeration of the Sciences*, Chapter 5.

[7] Not to mention the fact that the authors of the *Politics* and the *Cyropaedia* were "strangers" when they wrote those books. Cf. *Politics*, 1273b27-32.

guided by questions concerning the external relations of the political community. It is concerned primarily with the inner structure of the political community, because that inner structure is essentially the subject of such political controversy as essentially involves the danger of civil war.[8]

The actual conflict of groups struggling for political power within the community naturally gives rise to the question what group should rule, or what compromise would be the best solution—that is to say, what political order would be the best order. Either the opposed groups are merely factions made up of the same type of men (such as parties of noblemen or adherents of opposed dynasties), or each of the opposed groups represents a specific type. Only in the latter case does the political struggle go to the roots of political life; then it becomes apparent to everyone, from everyday political life, that the question as to what type of men should have the decisive say is the subject of the most fundamental political controversy.

The immediate concern of that controversy is the best political order for the given political community, but every answer to that immediate question implies an answer to the universal question of the best political order as such. It does not require the exertions of philosophers to lay bare this implication, for the political controversy has a natural tendency to express itself in universal terms. A man who rejects kingship for Israel cannot help using arguments against kingship as such; a man who defends democracy in Athens cannot help using arguments in favor of democracy as such. When they are confronted with the fact that monarchy is the best political order, say, for Babylon, the natural reaction of such men will be that this fact shows the inferiority of Babylon and not that the question of the best political order does not make sense.

The groups, or types, whose claims to rule were considered by the classical philosophers were "the good" (men of merit), the rich, the noble, and the multitude, or the poor citizens; in the foreground of the political scene in the Greek cities, as well as in other places, was the struggle between the rich and the poor. The claim to rule which is based on merit, on human excellence, on "virtue," appeared to be least controversial; courageous and skilful generals, incorruptible and equitable judges, wise and unselfish magistrates, are generally

---

[8] Aristotle, *Politics*, 1200b36-39; Rousseau, *Contrat social*, ii, 9.

preferred. Thus "aristocracy" (rule of the best) presented itself as the natural answer of all good men to the natural question of the best political order. As Thomas Jefferson put it, "That form of government is the best, which provides the most effectually for a pure selection of [the] natural *aristoi* into offices of the government." [9]

What is to be understood by "good men" was known also from political life: good men are those who are willing, and able, to prefer the common interest to their private interest and to the objects of their passions, or those who, being able to discern in each situation what is the noble or right thing to do, do it because it is noble and right and for no ulterior reason. It was also generally recognized that this answer gives rise to further questions of almost overwhelming political significance: that results which are generally considered desirable can be achieved by men of dubious character or by the use of unfair means; that "just" and "useful" are not simply identical; that virtue may lead to ruin.[10]

Thus the question guiding classical political philosophy, the typical answer that it gave, and the insight into the bearing of the formidable objections to it, belong to pre-philosophic political life, or precede political philosophy. Political philosophy goes beyond pre-philosophic political knowledge by trying to understand fully the implications of these pre-philosophic insights, and especially by defending the second of them against the more or less "sophisticated" attacks made by bad or perplexed men.

When the pre-philosophic answer is accepted, the most urgent question concerns the "materials" and institutions which would be most favorable to "the rule of the best." It is primarily by answering this question, by thus elaborating a "blueprint" of the best polity, that the political philosopher becomes the teacher of legislators. The legislator is strictly limited in his choice of institutions and laws by the character of the people for whom he legislates, by their traditions, by the nature of their territory, by their economic conditions, and so on. His choosing this or that law is normally a compromise between what he would wish and what circumstances permit. To effect that compromise intelligently, he must first know what he wishes, or,

[9] Letter to John Adams, October 28, 1813.
[10] See Aristotle, *Nicomachean Ethics*, 1094b18 ff.; Xenophon, *Memorabilia*, IV 2, 32 ff.

rather, what would be most desirable in itself. The political philosopher can answer that question because he is not limited in his reflections by any particular set of circumstances, but is free to choose the most favorable conditions that are possible—ethnic, climatic, economic, and other—and thus to determine what laws and institutions would be preferable under those conditions.[11] After that, he tries to bridge the gulf between what is most desirable in itself and what is possible in given circumstances, by discussing what polity, and what laws, would be best under various types of more or less unfavorable conditions, and even what kinds of laws and measures are appropriate for preserving any kind of polity, however defective. By thus erecting on the "normative" foundation of political science a "realistic" structure, or, to speak somewhat more adequately, by thus supplementing political physiology with political pathology and therapeutics, he does not retract or even qualify, he rather confirms, his view that the question of the best polity is necessarily the guiding question.[12]

By the best political order the classical philosopher understood that political order which is best always and everywhere.[13] This does not mean that he conceived of that order as necessarily good for every community, as "a perfect solution for all times and for every place": a given community may be so rude or so depraved that only a very inferior type of order can "keep it going." But it does mean that the goodness of the political order realized anywhere and at any time can be judged only in terms of that political order which is best absolutely. "The best political order" is, then, not intrinsically Greek: it is no more intrinsically Greek than health, as is shown by the parallelism of political science and medicine. But just as it may happen that the members of one nation are more likely to be healthy and strong than those of others, it may also happen that one nation has a greater natural fitness for political excellence than others.

When Aristotle asserted that the Greeks had a greater natural fitness for political excellence than the nations of the north and those of Asia, he did not assert, of course, that political excellence was

[11] See Aristotle, *Politics*, 1265a17 ff. and 1325b33-40; Plato, *Laws*, 857e8-858c3; Cicero, *Republic*, I, 33.

[12] See Plato, *Laws*, 739b8 ff., and the beginning of the fourth book of Aristotle's *Politics*.

[13] Aristotle, *Nicomachean Ethics*, 1135a4-5.

identical with the quality of being Greek or derivative from it; otherwise he could not have praised the institutions of Carthage as highly as the institutions of the most renowned Greek cities. When Socrates asked Glaucon in the *Republic* whether the city that Glaucon was founding would be a Greek city, and Glaucon answered emphatically in the affirmative, neither of them said any more than that a city founded by Greeks would necessarily be a Greek city. The purpose of this truism, or rather of Socrates' question, was to induce the warlike Glaucon to submit to a certain moderation of warfare: since a general prohibition of wars was not feasible, at least warfare among Greeks should keep within certain limits. The fact that a perfect city founded by Glaucon would be a Greek city does not imply that any perfect city was necessarily Greek: Socrates considered it possible that the perfect city, which certainly did not exist at that time anywhere in Greece, existed at that time "in some barbarian place." [14] Xenophon went so far as to describe the Persian Cyrus as *the* perfect ruler, and to imply that the education Cyrus received in Persia was superior even to Spartan education; and he did not consider it impossible that a man of the rank of Socrates would emerge among the Armenians.[15]

Because of its direct relation to political life classical political philosophy was essentially "practical"; on the other hand, it is no accident that modern political philosophy frequently calls itself political "theory." [16] The primary concern of the former was not the description, or understanding, of political life, but its right guidance. Hegel's demand that political philosophy refrain from construing a state as it ought to be, or from teaching the state how it should be, and that it try to understand the present and actual state as something essentially rational, amounts to a rejection of the *raison d'être* of classical political philosophy. In contrast with present-day political science, or with well-known interpretations of present-day political

---

[14] Plato, *Republic*, 427c2-3, 470e4 ff. and 499c7-9; see also *Laws*, 739c3 (compare *Republic*, 373e, with *Phaedo*, 78a3-5, and *Laws*, 656e-657b and 799a ff.; also *Minos*, 316d.

[15] *Cyropaedia*, I 1 and 2, III 1, 38-40; compare II 2, 26.

[16] Hegel, *Vorlesungen ueber die Geschichte der Philosophie*, ed. Michelet-Glockner, I, 291: "Wir werden ueberhaupt die praktische Philosophie nicht spekulativ werden sehen, bis auf die neuesten Zeiten." Cf. Schelling, *Studium Generale*, ed. Glockner, 94-95.

science, classical political philosophy pursued practical aims and was guided by, and culminated in, "value judgments." The attempt to replace the quest for the best political order by a purely descriptive or analytical political science which refrains from "value judgments" is, from the point of view of the classics, as absurd as the attempt to replace the art of making shoes, that is, good and well-fitting shoes, by a museum of shoes made by apprentices, or as the idea of a medicine which refuses to distinguish between health and sickness.

Since political controversies are concerned with "good things" and "just things," classical political philosophy was naturally guided by considerations of "goodness" and "justice." It started from the moral distinctions as they are made in everyday life, although it knew better than the dogmatic skeptic of our time the formidable theoretical objections to which they are exposed. Such distinctions as those between courage and cowardice, justice and injustice, human kindness and selfishness, gentleness and cruelty, urbanity and rudeness, are intelligible and clear for all practical purposes, that is, in most cases, and they are of decisive importance in guiding our lives: this is a sufficient reason for considering the fundamental political questions in their light.

In the sense in which these distinctions are politically relevant, they cannot be "demonstrated," they are far from being perfectly lucid, and they are exposed to grave theoretical doubts. Accordingly, classical political philosophy limited itself to addressing men who, because of their natural inclinations as well as their upbringing, took those distinctions for granted. It knew that one can perhaps silence but not truly convince such people as have no "taste" for the moral distinctions and their significance: not even Socrates himself could convert, though he could silence, such men as Meletus and Callicles, and he admitted the limits set to demonstrations in this sphere by taking recourse to "myths."

The political teaching of the classical philosophers, as distinguished from their theoretical teaching, was primarily addressed not to all intelligent men, but to all decent men.[17] A political teaching which addressed itself equally to decent and indecent men would have ap-

[17] See Aristotle, *Nicomachean Ethics*, 1095b4-6 and 1140b13-18; Cicero, *Laws*, I, 37-39.

peared to them from the outset as unpolitical, that is, as politically, or socially, irresponsible; for if it is true that the well-being of the political community requires that its members be guided by considerations of decency or morality, the political community cannot tolerate a political science which is morally "neutral" and which therefore tends to loosen the hold of moral principles on the minds of those who are exposed to it. To express the same view somewhat differently, even if it were true that when men are talking of right they are thinking only of their interests, it would be equally true that that reserve is of the essence of political man, and that by emancipating oneself from it one would cease to be a political man or to speak his language.

Thus the attitude of classical political philosophy toward political things was always akin to that of the enlightened statesman; it was not the attitude of the detached observer who looks at political things in the way in which a zoologist looks at the big fishes swallowing the small ones, or that of the social "engineer" who thinks in terms of manipulating or conditioning rather than in terms of education or liberation, or that of the prophet who believes that he knows the future.

In brief, the root of classical political philosophy was the fact that political life is characterized by controversies between groups struggling for power within the political community. Its purpose was to settle those political controversies which are of a fundamental and typical character in the spirit not of the partisan but of the good citizen, and with a view to such an order as would be most in accordance with the requirements of human excellence. Its guiding subject was the most fundamental politically controversial subject, understood in the way, and in the terms, in which it was understood in pre-philosophic political life.

In order to perform his function the philosopher had to raise an ulterior question which is never raised in the political arena. That question is so simple, elementary and unobtrusive that it is, at first, not even intelligible, as is shown by a number of occurrences described in the Platonic dialogues. This distinctly philosophic question is "What is virtue?" What is that virtue whose possession—as everyone admits spontaneously or is reduced to silence by unanswerable arguments—gives a man the highest right to rule? In the light of this question the common opinions about virtue appear at the outset as unconscious attempts to answer an unconscious question. On closer examination their radical insufficiency is more specifically revealed by the fact that some of them are contradicted by other opinions which are equally common. To reach consistency the philosopher is compelled to maintain one part of common opinion and to give up the other part which contradicts it; he is thus driven to adopt a view that is no longer generally held, a truly paradoxical view, one that is generally considered "absurd" or "ridiculous."

Nor is that all. He is ultimately compelled to transcend not merely the dimension of common opinion, of political opinion, but the dimension of political life as such; for he is led to realize that the ultimate aim of political life cannot be reached by political life, but only by a life devoted to contemplation, to philosophy. This finding is of crucial importance for political philosophy, since it determines the limits set to political life, to all political action and all political planning. Moreover, it implies that the highest subject of political philosophy is the philosophic life: philosophy—not as a teaching or as a body of knowledge, but as a way of life—offers, as it were, the solution to the problem that keeps political life in motion. Ultimately, political philosophy transforms itself into a discipline that is no longer concerned with political things in the ordinary sense of the term: Socrates called his inquiries a quest for "the *true* political skill," and Aristotle called his discussion of virtue and related subjects "a *kind* of political science." [18]

No difference between classical political philosophy and modern political philosophy is more telling than this: the philosophic life, or the life of "the wise," which was the highest subject of classical political philosophy, has in modern times almost completely ceased to be a subject of political philosophy. Yet even this ultimate step of classical political philosophy, however absurd it seemed to the common opinion, was nevertheless "divined" by pre-philosophic political life: men wholly devoted to the political life were sometimes popu-

[18] Plato, *Gorgias*, 521d7; Aristotle, *Nicomachean Ethics*, 1094b11 and 1130b26-29 (*Rhetoric*, 1356a25 f.).

larly considered "busybodies," and their unresting habits were contrasted with the greater freedom and the higher dignity of the more retired life of men who were "minding their own business." [19]

The direct relation of classical political philosophy to pre-philosophic political life was due not to the undeveloped character of classical philosophy or science, but to mature reflection. This reflection is summed up in Aristotle's description of political philosophy as "the philosophy concerning the human things." This description reminds us of the almost overwhelming difficulty which had to be overcome before philosophers could devote any serious attention to political things, to human things. The "human things" were distinguished from the "divine things" or the "natural things," and the latter were considered absolutely superior in dignity to the former.[20] Philosophy, therefore, was at first exclusively concerned with the natural things. Thus, in the beginning, philosophic effort was concerned only negatively, only accidentally, with political things. Socrates himself, the founder of political philosophy, was famous as a philosopher before he ever turned to political philosophy. Left to themselves, the philosophers would not descend again to the "cave" of political life, but would remain outside in what they considered "the island of the blessed"—contemplation of the truth.[21]

But philosophy, being an attempt to rise from opinion to science, is necessarily related to the sphere of opinion as its essential starting point, and hence to the political sphere. Therefore the political sphere is bound to advance into the focus of philosophic interest as soon as philosophy starts to reflect on its own doings. To understand fully its own purpose and nature, philosophy has to understand its essential starting-point, and hence the nature of political things.

The philosophers, as well as other men who have become aware of

[19] Aristotle, *Nicomachean Ethics*, 1142a1-2 (compare 1177a25 ff.), and *Metaphysics*, 982b25-28; Plato, *Republic*, 620c4-7 and 549c2 ff., and *Theaetetus*, 172c8 ff. and 173c8 ff. See also Xenophon, *Memorabilia*, I 2, 47 ff. and II 9, 1.

[20] Aristotle, *Nicomachean Ethics*, 1181b15, 1141a20-b9, 1155b2 ff., and 1177b30 ff. Compare the typical disagreement between the philosopher and the legislator in Plato's *Laws*, 804b5-cl, with his *Meno*, 94e3-4, and *Apologia Socratis*, 23a6-7 (also *Republic*, 517d4-5, *Theaetetus*, 175c5, and *Politicus*, 267e9 ff.). Compare also Xenophon, *Memorabilia*, I 1, 11-16. and Seneca, *Naturales Quaestiones*, I, beginning.

[21] Plato, *Republic*, 519b7-d7; compare *ibid.*, 521b7-10.

the possibility of philosophy, are sooner or later driven to wonder "Why philosophy?" Why does human life need philosophy, why is it good, why is it right, that opinions about the nature of the whole should be replaced by genuine knowledge of the nature of the whole? Since human life is living together or, more exactly, is political life, the question "Why philosophy?" means "Why does political life need philosophy?" This question calls philosophy before the tribunal of the political community: It makes philosophy politically responsible. Like Plato's perfect city itself, which, once established, does not permit the philosophers to devote themselves any longer exclusively to contemplation, this question, once raised, forbids the philosophers any longer to disregard political life altogether. Plato's *Republic* as a whole, as well as other political works of the classical philosophers, can best be described as an attempt to supply a political justification for philosophy by showing that the well-being of the political community depends decisively on the study of philosophy. Such a justification was all the more urgent since the meaning of philosophy was by no means generally understood, and hence philosophy was distrusted and hated by many well-meaning citizens.[22] Socrates himself fell victim to the popular prejudice against philosophy.

To justify philosophy before the tribunal of the political community means to justify philosophy in terms of the political community, that is to say, by means of a kind of argument which appeals not to philosophers as such, but to citizens as such. To prove to citizens that philosophy is permissible, desirable or even necessary, the philosopher has to follow the example of Odysseus and start from premises that are generally agreed upon, or from generally accepted opinions:[23] he has to argue *ad hominem* or "dialectically." From this point of view the adjective "political" in the expression "political philosophy" designates not so much a subject matter as a manner of treatment;[24] from this point of view, I say, "political philosophy"

---

[22] Plato, *Republic*, 520b2-3 and 494a4-10, *Phaedo*, 64b, and *Apologia Socratis*, 23d1-7. Compare Cicero, *Tusculanae disputationes*, II 1, 4, and *De officiis*, II 1, 2, and Plutarch, *Nicias*, 23.

[23] Xenophon, *Memorabilia*, IV 6, 15.

[24] Aristotle, *Politics*, 1275b25 (compare J. F. Gronovius' note to Grotius, *De pure belli*, Prolegomena, § 44) and *Nicomachean Ethics*, 1171a15-20; Polybius,

means primarily not the philosophic treatment of politics, but the political, or popular, treatment of philosophy, or the political introduction to philosophy—the attempt to lead the qualified citizens, or rather their qualified sons, from the political life to the philosophic life. This deeper meaning of "political philosophy" tallies well with its ordinary meaning, for in both cases "political philosophy" culminates in praise of the philosophic life. At any rate, it is ultimately because he means to justify philosophy before the tribunal of the political community, and hence on the level of political discussion, that the philosopher has to understand the political things exactly as they are understood in political life.

In his political philosophy the philosopher starts, then, from that understanding of political things which is natural to pre-philosophic political life. At the beginning the fact that a certain habitual attitude or a certain way of acting is generally praised, is a sufficient reason for considering that attitude, or that way of acting, a virtue. But the philosopher is soon compelled, or able, to transcend the dimension of pre-philosophic understanding by raising the crucial question "What is virtue?" The attempt to answer this question leads to a critical distinction between the generally praised attitudes which are rightly praised, and those which are not; and it leads to the recognition of a certain hierarchy, unknown in pre-philosophic life, of the different virtues. Such a philosophic critique of the generally accepted views is at the bottom of the fact that Aristotle, for example, omitted piety and sense of shame from his list of virtues,[25] and that his list starts with courage and moderation (the least intellectual virtues) and, proceeding via liberality, magnanimity, and the virtues of private relations, to justice, culminates in the dianoetic virtues.[26] Moreover, insight into the limits of the moral-political sphere as a whole can be expounded fully only by answering

---

v 33.5; see also Locke, *Essay Concerning Human Understanding*, III, 9, §§ 3 and 22. Note especially the derogatory meaning of "political" in the term "political virtue": Plato, *Phaedo*, 82a10 ff., and *Republic*, 430c3-5, and Aristotle, *Nicomachean Ethics*, 1116a17 ff.

[25] *Eudemian Ethics*, 1221a1.

[26] *Nicomachean Ethics*, 1117b23 ff., and *Rhetoric*, I 5, 6. See also Plato, *Laws*, 630c ff. and 963e, and *Phaedrus*, 247d5-7; Xenophon, *Memorabilia*, IV 8, 11 (compare his *Apologia Socratis*, 14-16); Thomas Aquinas, *Summa theologica*, 2, 2, qu. 129 art. 2 and qu. 58 art. 12.

the question of the nature of political things. This question marks the limit of political philosophy as a practical discipline: while essentially practical in itself, the question functions as an entering wedge for others whose purpose is no longer to guide action but simply to understand things as they are.[27]

[27] See, for example, Aristotle, *Politics*, 1258b8 ff., 1279b11 ff., and 1299a28 ff.

PLATO'S THEORY OF IDEAS

Bertrand Russell

The middle of the *Republic*, from the later part of Book V
to the end of Book VII, is occupied mainly with questions of pure
philosophy, as opposed to politics. These questions are introduced
by a somewhat abrupt statement:

> Until philosophers are kings, or the kings and princes of this
> world have the spirit and power of philosophy, and political
> greatness and wisdom meet in one, and those commoner natures
> who pursue either to the exclusion of the other are compelled
> to stand aside, cities will never have rest from these evils—no,
> nor the human race, as I believe—and then only will this our
> State have a possibility of life and behold the light of day.

If this is true, we must decide what constitutes a philosopher, and
what we mean by "philosophy." The consequent discussion is the
most famous part of the *Republic*, and has perhaps been the most
influential. It has, in parts, extraordinary literary beauty; the reader
may disagree (as I do) with what is said, but cannot help being
moved by it.

Bertrand Russell *is Fellow of Trinity College, Cambridge, a distin-
guished philosopher and mathematician, and winner of the Nobel
Prize for Literature. "Plato's Theory of Ideas" is chapter XV of his*
A History of Western Philosophy (*New York: Simon and Schuster,
Inc., 1945*). *Copyright 1945 by Bertrand Russell. Reprinted by per-
mission of Simon and Schuster, Inc. and George Allen & Unwin Ltd.*

Plato's philosophy rests on the distinction between reality and appearance, which was first set forth by Parmenides; throughout the discussion with which we are now concerned, Parmenidean phrases and arguments are constantly recurring. There is, however, a religious tone about reality, which is rather Pythagorean than Parmenidean; and there is much about mathematics and music which is directly traceable to the disciples of Pythagoras. This combination of the logic of Parmenides with the other-worldliness of Pythagoras and the Orphics produced a doctrine which was felt to be satisfying to both the intellect and the religious emotions; the result was a very powerful synthesis, which, with various modifications, influenced most of the great philosophers, down to and including Hegel. But not only philosophers were influenced by Plato. Why did the Puritans object to the music and painting and gorgeous ritual of the Catholic Church? You will find the answer in the tenth book of the *Republic*. Why are children in school compelled to learn arithmetic? The reasons are given in the seventh book.

The following paragraphs summarize Plato's theory of ideas.

Our question is: What is a philosopher? The first answer is in accordance with the etymology: a philosopher is a lover of wisdom. But this is not the same thing as a lover of knowledge, in the sense in which an inquisitive man may be said to love knowledge; vulgar curiosity does not make a philosopher. The definition is therefore amended: the philosopher is a man who loves the "vision of truth." But what is this vision?

Consider a man who loves beautiful things, who makes a point of being present at new tragedies, seeing new pictures, and hearing new music. Such a man is not a philosopher, because he loves only beautiful things, whereas the philosopher loves beauty in itself. The man who only loves beautiful things is dreaming, whereas the man who knows absolute beauty is wide awake. The former has only opinion; the latter has knowledge.

What is the difference between "knowledge" and "opinion"? The man who has knowledge has knowledge of *something*, that is to say, of something that exists, for what does not exist is nothing. (This is reminiscent of Parmenides.) Thus knowledge is infallible, since it is logically impossible for it to be mistaken. But opinion can be mistaken. How can this be? Opinion cannot be of what is not, for that is impossible; nor of what is, for then it would be knowledge. Therefore opinion must be of what both is and is not.

But how is this possible? The answer is that particular things always partake of opposite characters: what is beautiful is also, in some respects, ugly; what is just is, in some respects, unjust; and so on. All particular sensible objects, so Plato contends, have this contradictory character; they are thus intermediate between being and not-being, and are suitable as objects of opinion, but not of knowledge. "But those who see the absolute and eternal and immutable may be said to know, and not to have opinion only."

Thus we arrive at the conclusion that opinion is of the world presented to the senses, whereas knowledge is of a super-sensible eternal world; for instance, opinion is concerned with particular beautiful things, but knowledge is concerned with beauty in itself.

The only argument advanced is that it is self-contradictory to suppose that a thing can be both beautiful and not beautiful, or both just and not just, and that nevertheless particular things seem to combine such contradictory characters. Therefore particular things are not real. Heraclitus had said "We step and do not step into the same rivers; we are and are not." By combining this with Parmenides we arrive at Plato's result.

There is, however, something of great importance in Plato's doctrine which is not traceable to his predecessors, and that is the theory of "ideas" or "forms." This theory is partly logical, partly metaphysical. The logical part has to do with the meaning of general words. There are many individual animals of whom we can truly say "this is a cat." What do we mean by the word "cat"? Obviously something different from each particular cat. An animal is a cat, it would seem, because it participates in a general nature common to all cats. Language cannot get on without general words such as "cat," and such words are evidently not something which is not this or that cat, but some kind of universal cattiness. This is not born when a particular cat is born, and does not die when it dies. In fact, it has no position in space or time; it is "eternal." This is the logical part of the doctrine. The arguments in its favor, whether ultimately valid or not, are strong, and quite independent of the metaphysical part of the doctrine.

According to the metaphysical part of the doctrine, the word "cat" means a certain ideal cat, "*the* cat," created by God, and unique. Particular cats partake of the nature of *the* cat, but more or less imperfectly; it is only owing to this imperfection that there can be many of them. *The* cat is real; particular cats are only *apparent*.

In the last book of the *Republic*, as a preliminary to a condemnation of painters, there is a very clear exposition of the doctrine of ideas or forms.

Here Plato explains that, whenever a number of individuals have a common name, they have also a common "idea" or "form." For instance, though there are many beds, there is only one "idea" or "form" of a bed. Just as a reflection of a bed in a mirror is only apparent and not "real," so the various particular beds are unreal, being only copies of the "idea," which is the one real bed, and is made by God. Of this one bed, made by God, there can be *knowledge*, but in respect of the many beds made by carpenters there can be only *opinion*. The philosopher, as such, will be interested only in the one ideal bed, not in the many beds found in the sensible world. He will have a certain indifference to ordinary mundane affairs: "how can he who has magnificence of mind and is the spectator of all time and all existence, think much of human life?" The youth who is capable of becoming a philosopher will be distinguished among his fellows as just and gentle, fond of learning, possessed of a good memory and a naturally harmonious mind. Such a one shall be educated into a philosopher and a guardian.

At this point Adeimantus breaks in with a protest. When he tries to argue with Socrates, he says, he feels himself led a little astray at each step, until, in the end, all his former notions are turned upside down. But whatever Socrates may say, it remains the case, as any one can see, that people who stick to philosophy become strange monsters, not to say utter rogues; even the best of them are made useless by philosophy.

Socrates admits that this is true in the world as it is, but maintains that it is the other people who are to blame, not the philosophers; in a wise community the philosophers would not seem foolish; it is only among fools that the wise are judged to be destitute of wisdom.

What are we to do in this dilemma? There were to have been two ways of inaugurating our Republic: by philosophers becoming rulers, or by rulers becoming philosophers. The first way seems impossible as a beginning, because in a city not already philosophic the philosophers are unpopular. But a born prince *might* be a philosopher, and "one is enough; let there be one man who has a city obedient to his will, and he might bring into existence the ideal polity about which the world is so incredulous." Plato hoped that he had found such a prince in the younger Dionysius, tyrant of Syracuse, but the young man turned out disappointingly.

In the sixth and seventh books of the *Republic*, Plato is concerned with two questions: First, what is philosophy? Second, how can a young man or woman, of suitable temperament, be so educated as to become a philosopher?

Philosophy, for Plato, is a kind of vision, the "vision of truth." It is not *purely* intellectual; it is not merely wisdom, but *love* of wisdom. Spinoza's "intellectual love of God" is much the same intimate union of thought and feeling. Every one who has done any kind of creative work has experienced, in a greater or less degree, the state of mind in which, after long labor, truth or beauty appears, or seems to appear, in a sudden glory—it may be only about some small matter, or it may be about the universe. The experience is, at the moment, very convincing; doubt may come later, but at the time there is utter certainty. I think most of the best creative work, in art, in science, in literature, and in philosophy, has been the result of such a moment. Whether it comes to others as to me, I cannot say. For my part, I have found that, when I wish to write a book on some subject, I must first soak myself in detail, until all the separate parts of the subject-matter are familiar; then, some day, if I am fortunate, I perceive the whole, with all its parts duly interrelated. After that, I only have to write down what I have seen. The nearest analogy is first walking all over a mountain in a mist, until every path and ridge and valley is separately familiar, and then, from a distance, seeing the mountain whole and clear in bright sunshine.

This experience, I believe, is necessary to good creative work, but it is not sufficient; indeed the subjective certainty that it brings with it may be fatally misleading. William James describes a man who got the experience from laughing-gas; whenever he was under its influence, he knew the secret of the universe, but when he came to, he had forgotten it. At last, with immense effort, he wrote down the secret before the vision had faded. When completely recovered, he rushed to see what he had written. It was: "A smell of petroleum prevails throughout." What seems like sudden insight may be misleading, and must be tested soberly, when the divine intoxication has passed.

Plato's vision, which he completely trusted at the time when he wrote the *Republic*, needs ultimately the help of a parable, the parable of the cave, in order to convey its nature to the reader. But it is led up to by various preliminary discussions, designed to make the reader see the necessity of the world of ideas.

First, the world of the intellect is distinguished from the world of the senses; then intellect and sense-perception are in turn each divided into two kinds. The two kinds of sense-perception need not concern us; the two kinds of intellect are called, respectively, "reason" and "understanding." Of these, reason is the higher kind; it is concerned with pure ideas, and its method is dialectic. Understanding is the kind of intellect that is used in mathematics; it is inferior to reason in that it uses hypotheses which it cannot test. In geometry, for example, we say: "Let ABC be a rectilinear triangle." It is against the rules to ask whether ABC really *is* a rectilinear triangle, although, if it is a figure that we have drawn, we may be sure that it is not, because we can't draw absolutely straight lines. Accordingly, mathematics can never tell us what *is*, but only what *would* be if. . . . There are no straight lines in the sensible world; therefore, if mathematics is to have more than hypothetical truth, we must find evidence for the existence of super-sensible straight lines in a super-sensible world. This cannot be done by the understanding, but according to Plato it can be done by reason, which shows that there is a rectilinear triangle in heaven, of which geometrical propositions can be affirmed categorically, not hypothetically.

There is, at this point, a difficulty which did not escape Plato's notice, and was evident to modern idealistic philosophers. We saw that God made only one bed, and it would be natural to suppose that he made only one straight line. But if there is a heavenly triangle, he must have made at least three straight lines. The objects of geometry, though ideal, must exist in many examples; we need the possibility of *two* intersecting circles, and so on. This suggests that geometry, on Plato's theory, should not be capable of ultimate truth, but should be condemned as part of the study of appearance. We will, however, ignore this point, as to which Plato's answer is somewhat obscure.

Plato seeks to explain the difference between clear intellectual vision and the confused vision of sense-perception by an analogy from the sense of sight. Sight, he says, differs from the other senses, since it requires not only the eye and the object, but also light. We see clearly objects on which the sun shines: in twilight we see confusedly, and in pitch-darkness not at all. Now the world of ideas is what we see when the object is illumined by the sun, while the world of passing things is a confused twilight world. The eye is compared to the soul, and the sun, as the source of light, to truth or goodness.

> The soul is like an eye: when resting upon that on which truth and being shine, the soul perceives and understands, and is radiant with intelligence; but when turned toward the twilight of becoming and perishing, when she has opinion only, and goes blinking about, and is first of one opinion and then of another, and seems to have no intelligence. . . . Now what imparts truth to the known and the power of knowing to the knower is what I would have you term the idea of good, and this you will deem to be the cause of science.

This leads up to the famous simile of the cave or den, according to which those who are destitute of philosophy may be compared to prisoners in a cave, who are only able to look in one direction because they are bound, and who have a fire behind them and a wall in front. Between them and the wall there is nothing; all that they see are shadows of themselves, and of objects behind them, cast on the wall by the light of the fire. Inevitably they regard these shadows as real, and have no notion of the objects to which they are due. At last some man succeeds in escaping from the cave to the light of the sun; for the first time he sees real things, and becomes aware that he had hitherto been deceived by shadows. If he is the sort of philosopher who is fit to become a guardian, he will feel it his duty to those who were formerly his fellow-prisoners to go down again into the cave, instruct them as to the truth, and show them the way up. But he will have difficulty in persuading them, because, coming out of the sunlight, he will see shadows less clearly than they do, and will seem to them stupider than before his escape.

> "And now, I said, let me show in a figure how far our nature is enlightened or unenlightened:—Behold! human beings living in an underground den, which has a mouth open toward the light and reaching all along the den; here they have been from their childhood, and have their legs and necks chained so that they cannot move, and can only see before them, being prevented by the chains from turning round their heads. Above and behind them a fire is blazing at a distance, and between the fire and the prisoners there is a raised way; and you will see, if you look, a low wall built along the way, like the screen which marionette players have in front of them, over which they show the puppets.
>
> "I see.
>
> "And do you see, I said, men passing along the wall carrying all sorts of vessels, and statues and figures of animals made of wood and stone and various materials, which appear over the wall? Some of them are talking, others silent.
>
> "You have shown me a strange image, and they are strange prisoners.
>
> "Like ourselves, I replied; and they see only their own shadows, or the shadows of one another, which the fire throws on the opposite wall of the cave."

The position of the good in Plato's philosophy is peculiar. Science and truth, he says, are *like* the good, but the good has a higher place. "The good is not essence, but far exceeds essence in dignity and power." Dialectic leads to the end of the intellectual world in the perception of the absolute good. It is by means of the good that dialectic is able to dispense with the hypotheses of the mathematician. The underlying assumption is that reality, as opposed to appearance, is completely and perfectly good; to perceive the good, therefore, is to perceive reality. Throughout Plato's philosophy there is the same fusion of intellect and mysticism as in Pythagoreanism, but at this final culmination mysticism clearly has the upper hand.

Plato's doctrine of ideas contains a number of obvious errors. But in spite of these it marks a very important advance in philosophy, since it is the first theory to emphasize the problem of universals, which, in varying forms, has persisted to the present day. Beginnings are apt to be crude, but their originality should not be overlooked on this account. Something remains of what Plato had to say, even after all necessary corrections have been made. The absolute minimum of what remains, even in the view of those most hostile to Plato, is this: that we cannot express ourselves in a language composed wholly of proper names, but must have also general words such as "man," "dog," "cat"; or, if not these, then relational words such as "similar," "before," and so on. Such words are not meaningless noises, and it is difficult to see how they can have meaning if the world consists entirely of particular things, such as are designated by proper names. There may be ways of getting round this argument, but at any rate it affords a *prima facie* case in favor of universals. I shall provisionally accept it as in some degree valid. But when so much is granted, the rest of what Plato says by no means follows.

In the first place, Plato has no understanding of philosophical syntax. I can say "Socrates is human," "Plato is human," and so on. In all these statements, it may be assumed that the word "human" has exactly the same meaning. But whatever it means, it means something which is not of the same kind as Socrates, Plato, and the rest of the individuals who compose the human race. "Human" is an adjective; it would be nonsense to say "human is human." Plato makes a mistake analogous to saying "human is human." He thinks that beauty is beautiful; he thinks that the universal "man" is the name of a pattern man created by God, of whom actual men are imperfect and somewhat unreal copies. He fails altogether to realize how great is the gap between universals and particulars; his "ideas" are really just other particulars, ethically and aesthetically superior to the ordinary kind. He himself, at a later date, began to see this difficulty, as appears in the *Parmenides*, which contains one of the most remarkable cases in history of self-criticism by a philosopher.

The *Parmenides* is supposed to be related by Antiphon (Plato's half-brother), who alone remembers the conversation, but is now only interested in horses. They find him carrying a bridle, and with difficulty persuade him to relate the famous discussion between Parmenides, Zeno, and Socrates. This, we are told, took place when Parmenides was old (about sixty-five), Zeno in middle life (about forty), and Socrates quite a young man. Socrates expounds the theory of ideas; he is sure that there are ideas of likeness, justice, beauty, and goodness; he is not sure that there is an idea of man; and he rejects with indignation the suggestion that there could be ideas of such things as hair and mud and dirt—though, he adds, there are times when he thinks that there is nothing without an idea. He runs away from this view because he is afraid of falling into a bottomless pit of nonsense.

"Yes, Socrates," said Parmenides; "that is because you are still young; the time will come, if I am not mistaken, when philosophy will have a firmer grasp of you, and then you will not despise even the meanest things."

Socrates agrees that, in his view, "There are certain ideas of which all other things partake, and from which they derive their names; that similars, for example, become similar, because they partake of similarity; and great things become great, because they partake of greatness; and that just and beautiful things become just and beautiful, because they partake of justice and beauty."

Parmenides proceeds to raise difficulties. (a) Does the individual partake of the whole idea, or only of a part? To either view there are objections. If the former, one thing is in many places at once; if the latter, the idea is divisible, and a thing which has a part of smallness will be smaller than absolute smallness, which is absurd. (b) When an individual partakes of an idea, the individual and the idea are similar; therefore there will have to be another idea, embracing both the particulars and the original idea. And there will have to be yet another, embracing the particulars and the two ideas, and so on *ad infinitum*. Thus every idea, instead of being one, becomes an infinite series of ideas. (This is the same as Aristotle's argument of the "third man.") (c) Socrates suggests that perhaps ideas are only thoughts, but Parmenides points out that thoughts must be *of* something. (d) Ideas cannot resemble the particulars that partake of them, for the reason given in (b) above. (e) Ideas, if there are any, must be unknown to us, because our knowledge is not absolute. (f) If God's knowledge is absolute, He will not know us, and therefore cannot rule us.

Nevertheless, the theory of ideas is not wholly abandoned. Without ideas, Socrates says, there will be nothing on which the mind can rest, and therefore reasoning will be destroyed. Parmenides tells him that his troubles come of lack of previous training, but no definite conclusion is reached.

I do not think that Plato's logical objections to the reality of sensible particulars will bear examination. He says, for example, that whatever is beautiful is also in some respects ugly; what is double is also half; and so on. But when we say of some work of art that it is beautiful in some respects and ugly in others, analysis will always (at least theoretically) enable us to say "this part or aspect is beautiful, while that part or aspect is ugly." And as regards "double" and "half," these are relative terms; there is no contradiction in the fact that 2 is double of 1 and half of 4. Plato is perpetually getting into trouble through not understanding relative terms. He thinks that if A is greater than B and less than C, then A is at once great and small, which seems to him a contradiction. Such troubles are among the infantile diseases of philosophy.

The distinction between reality and appearance cannot have the consequences attributed to it by Parmenides and Plato and Hegel. If appearance really appears, it is not nothing, and is therefore part of reality; this is an argument of the correct Parmenidean sort. If appearance does not really appear, why trouble our heads about it? But perhaps some one will say: "Appearance does not really appear, but it appears to appear." This will not help, for we shall ask again: "Does it really appear to appear, or only *apparently* appear to appear?" Sooner or later, if appearance is even to appear to appear, we must reach something that *really* appears, and is therefore part of reality. Plato would not dream of denying that there appear to be many beds, although there is only one real bed, namely the one made by God. But he does not seem to have faced the implications of the fact that there are many appearances, and that this many-ness is part of reality. Any attempt to divide the world into portions, of which one is more "real" than the other, is doomed to failure.

Connected with this is another curious view of Plato's, that knowledge and opinion must be concerned with different subject-matters. We should say: If I think it is going to snow, that is opinion; if later I see it snowing, that is knowledge; but the subject-matter is the same on both occasions. Plato, however, thinks that what can at any time be a matter of opinion can never be a matter of knowledge. Knowledge is certain and infallible; opinion is not merely fallible, but is

necessarily mistaken, since it assumes the reality of what is only appearance. All this repeats what had been said by Parmenides.

There is one respect in which Plato's metaphysic is apparently different from that of Parmenides. For Parmenides there is only the
One; for Plato, there are many ideas. There are not only beauty,
truth, and goodness, but, as we saw, there is the heavenly bed, created
by God; there is a heavenly man, a heavenly dog, a heavenly cat, and
so on through a whole Noah's ark. All this however, seems, in the
Republic, to have been not adequately thought out. A Platonic idea
or form is not a thought, though it may be the object of a thought.
It is difficult to see how God can have created it, since its being is
timeless, and he could not have decided to create a bed unless his
thought, when he decided, had had for its object that very Platonic
bed which we are told he brought into existence. What is timeless
must be uncreated. We come here to a difficulty which has troubled
many philosophic theologians. Only the contingent world, the world
in space and time, can have been created; but this is the everyday
world which has been condemned as illusory and also bad. Therefore
the Creator, it would seem, created only illusion and evil. Some Gnos-
tics were so consistent as to adopt this view; but in Plato the difficulty
is still below the surface, and he seems, in the *Republic*, to have
never become aware of it.

The philosopher who is to be a guardian must, according to Plato,
return into the cave, and live among those who have never seen the
sun of truth. It would seem that God Himself, if He wishes to amend
His creation, must do likewise; a Christian Platonist might so interpret the Incarnation. But it remains completely impossible to explain
why God was not content with the world of ideas. The philosopher
finds the cave in existence, and is actuated by benevolence in returning to it; but the Creator, if He created everything, might, one would
think, have avoided the cave altogether.

Perhaps this difficulty arises only from the Christian notion of a
Creator, and is not chargeable to Plato, who says that God did not
create everything, but only what is good. The multiplicity of the
sensible world, on this view, would have some other source than God.
And the ideas would, perhaps, be not so much *created* by God as
constituents of His essence. The apparent pluralism involved in the
multiplicity of ideas would thus not be ultimate. Ultimately there is

only God, or the Good, to whom the ideas are adjectival. This, at any rate, is a possible interpretation of Plato.

Plato proceeds to an interesting sketch of the education proper to a young man who is to be a guardian. We saw that the young man is selected for this honor on the ground of a combination of intellectual and moral qualities; he must be just and gentle, fond of learning, with a good memory and a harmonious mind. The young man who has been chosen for these merits will spend the years from twenty to thirty on the four Pythagorean studies: arithmetic, geometry (plane and solid), astronomy, and harmony. These studies are not to be pursued in any utilitarian spirit, but in order to prepare his mind for the vision of eternal things. In astronomy, for example, he is not to trouble himself too much about the actual heavenly bodies, but rather with the mathematics of the motion of ideal heavenly bodies. This may sound absurd to modern ears, but, strange to say, it proved to be a fruitful point of view in connection with empirical astronomy. The way this came about is curious, and worth considering.

The apparent motions of the planets, until they have been very profoundly analyzed, appear to be irregular and complicated, and not at all such as a Pythagorean Creator would have chosen. It was obvious to every Greek that the heavens ought to exemplify mathematical beauty, which would be the case only if the planets moved in circles. This would be especially evident to Plato, owing to his emphasis on the good. The problem thus arose: Is there any hypothesis which will reduce the apparent disorderliness of planetary motions to order and beauty and simplicity? If there is, the idea of the good will justify us in asserting this hypothesis. Aristarchus of Samos found such a hypothesis: that all the planets, including the earth, go round the sun in circles. This view was rejected for two thousand years, partly on the authority of Aristotle, who attributes a rather similar hypothesis to "the Pythagoreans" (*De Coelo*, 293 *a*). It was revived by Copernicus, and its success might seem to justify Plato's aesthetic bias in astronomy. Unfortunately, however, Kepler discovered that the planets move in ellipses, not in circles, with the sun at a focus, not at the center; then Newton discovered that they do not move even in exact ellipses. And so the geometrical simplicity sought by Plato, and apparently found by Aristarchus of Samos, proved in the end illusory.

This piece of scientific history illustrates a general maxim: that any hypothesis, however absurd, *may* be useful in science, if it enables a discoverer to conceive things in a new way; but that, when it has served this purpose by luck, it is likely to become an obstacle to further advance. The belief in the good as the key to the scientific understanding of the world was useful, at a certain stage, in astronomy, but at every later stage it was harmful. The ethical and aesthetic bias of Plato, and still more of Aristotle, did much to kill Greek science.

It is noteworthy that modern Platonists, with few exceptions, are ignorant of mathematics, in spite of the immense importance that Plato attached to arithmetic and geometry, and the immense influence that they had on his philosophy. This is an example of the evils of specialization: a man must not write on Plato unless he has spent so much of his youth on Greek as to have had no time for the things that Plato thought important.

SOME OTHER SPECTRUM BOOKS

* Also available in limited clothbound edition.

The American Assembly Series

In the Classics in History Series

* Also available in limited clothbound edition.